NATHAN FIELD,
THE ACTOR-PLAYWRIGHT

BY

ROBERTA FLORENCE BRINKLEY

Archon Books

1973

Library of Congress Cataloging in Publication Data

Brinkley, Roberta Florence.
   Nathan Field, the actor-playwright.

     Original ed. issued as v. 77 of Yale studies in English.
     Original presented as the author's thesis, Yale, 1924.
     1. Field, Nathan, 1587—1620? I. Series: Yale studies
in English, v. 77.
PR2499.F4B7   1973   822'.3   72-8822
ISBN 0-208-01124-2

[Yale Studies in English, vol. 77]

Printed in the United States of America

PREFACE

The necessity for a study of Nathan Field, the actor-playwright, has developed because of the increasing tendency to attribute to him either the revision of plays or the composition of such portions of collaborative drama, 1613-19, as cannot be identified.

I wish to express my appreciation for the assistance given me in the preparation of this monograph by the various members of the staffs of Yale and Harvard libraries and of the British Museum. It is a pleasure to record my thanks to C. E. Simons, Record Searcher, Somerset House, London, for his suggestions of possible sources of new biographical material, and for his work in making transcriptions of documents. I am also indebted to various church officials for permission to search the records at St. Giles, Cripplegate; St. Giles-in-the-Fields; and Southwark Cathedral.

I desire to acknowledge the valuable aid of the late Professor Albert S. Cook in editing the first chapter of this work. To Professor Tucker Brooke I am indebted not only for rereading the manuscript in preparation for the press but also for the suggestion of the subject of this thesis and for guidance and encouragement in my investigation. To acknowledge my gratitude to him is but to voice a feeling shared by all who work under his direction.

GOUCHER COLLEGE,
October, 1927.

CONTENTS

NATHAN FIELD
THE ACTOR-PLAYWRIGHT

CHAPTER I

THE FAMILY AND EARLY LIFE OF NATHAN FIELD

Nathan Field, the actor-playwright, belonged to an old and distinguished family. Burke[1] says that the Field family was originally native to Alsace, and that the Counts de la Field lived at the Château de la Field near Colmar. The first member of the family in England, Hubertus de la Field, was granted extensive tracts of land in Lancaster by William the Conqueror, with whom he probably came over to England. The Fields seem always to have been leading citizens in the communities in which they resided, but two names in the line of the actor's family stand out in especial prominence:[2] John Field of Ardsley in Yorkshire was a noted astronomer; Richard Field from Hertfordshire was a prominent divine, and the author of an important treatise in five books called *Of the Church*.

The Fields were Oxford and Cambridge graduates. Richard Field, the divine, held four degrees, and his son, Nathaniel, was Oxford B.A. and M.A.[3] John Field, the

---

[1] J. B. Burke, *Landed Gentry* (London, 1851), de la Field.

[2] I was able to trace these connections through the similarity of the coat of arms (see appendix). The coat of arms used by Theophilus Field, Nathan's brother, was 'sable, a chevron between three garbs or' (F. T. Havergal, Fasti Herfordenses, Edinburgh, 1869, p. 173), the same as that of the noted astronomer, except for a crest which was granted as a reward for publishing the first astronomical tables based upon the Copernican system. The coat of arms of the divine had no chevron, but the chevron was often used to distinguish a different branch of the same family.

[3] J. Foster, *Alumni Oxonienses* (London, 1891) 2. 489.

astronomer, was thought by Wood to have been an Oxford graduate.[4]   The father of Nathan was an Oxford man,[5] and his son, Theophilus, was incorporated at Oxford as B.D. and D.D., after receiving two academic degrees from Cambridge.[6] Two of the sons of Theophilus were graduates from Oxford and Cambridge, respectively.   These Oxford and Cambridge men were a family of writers.   John Field, the astronomer, produced a number of publications of great importance; Richard Field, the divine, wrote books which have been a permanent contribution to church-history; and his son, Nathaniel, wrote a very interesting biography of his father, with some account of the family.[7]   The father of the actor and dramatist was an even more copious writer.   His tracts show the ability to think clearly and logically, and the power to express himself directly and with force.   His original productions were all either controversial in nature, or of such practical value as the little volume entitled 'Praiers and Meditations for the use of private families, and sundry other persons, according to their divers states and occasions.' He also made a number of translations from the French, chiefly of prayers and sermons by Calvin, or of other religious treatises.   Nathan's brother, Theophilus, was a writer as well as cleric.   His works are chiefly sermons, but he seems to have made some excursions into the realm of poetry.[8]

It is not until 1570 that we know positively the location of the Field family in which our immediate interest lies.   In

[4] Anthony à Wood, *Athenæ Oxonienses* (London, 1813-20) 1. 300.
[5] *Ibid.*, pp. 534-6.
[6] Foster, *op. cit.* 490.
[7] N. Field, *Some Short Memorials Concerning the Life of the Reverend Divine Doctor Field, Prebendary of Windsor and Dean of Glocester. The Learned Author of* 'Five Books of the Church' (London, 1716-7).
[8] Wood, *op. cit.* 2. 397. See also Thomas Corser, *Collectanea Anglo-Poetica* (Chetham Society, Manchester, 1780), CVIII, Part X, 1, pp. 248-51.

that year the baptism of John Field's first child was recorded in the baptismal register of St. Giles, Cripplegate. By 1572 John Field's name had become prominent in London, for he had become the recognized leader of those who were seeking a reformation in the church of England.

John Field felt so strongly in regard to the abuses of the church-forms that he became an important figure in the opening of the Marprelate controversy, though he did not live to see the first tract published. His position as instigator of this movement, and leader of the Puritans, has not been sufficiently taken into account, or estimated at its real value. When the Puritans gave up hope of securing a reformation through the influence of Queen Elizabeth, or through the bishops themselves, they turned to Parliament with an account of the abuses which were to be found within the church, and the immorality existing among its officials. An *Admonition to Parliament* was drawn up and presented by Field, then minister of Aldermary, London, and Thomas Wilcox. This document is severe in tone, for the authors did not hesitate to say that unless the abuses 'be removed and the truth brought in not only God's justice shall be poured forth, but also God's church in this realm shall never be builded.'[9] Field dealt too harshly with the bishops for his own good. By their influence both he and Wilcox were thrown into Newgate prison on October 2. After three months' imprisonment had passed, they were visited by the archbishop's chaplain, who reproved them for what he termed the abuse of the bishops. Field's answer was: 'This concerns me; the Scriptures of the Old and New Testament use such vehemency; we have used gentle words too long, which have done no good; the wound grows desperate and wants a corrosive; 'tis no time to blanch or sew

[9] J. Field and T. Wilcox, *Admonition to Parliament* (London, 1572), p. [6 m-n].

pillows under men's elbows, but God knoweth we meant
to touch no man's person but their places and abuses.'[10]
Neal reports that the conference began with a suitable prayer
by Field, and 'was carried on with such decency as moved
the Chaplain's compassion,' but Elizabeth's Ecclesiastical
Commission was not touched. The prisoners then composed
'an elegant Latin apology to the Lord Treasurer Burleigh,'
but nothing came of their efforts. On December 4, 1572,
they sent out from Newgate an orthodox confession of faith.
This was addressed 'Unto an Honorable and Vertuous Ladie,'
and was written partly at her request and partly 'to cleare
our selves of the vncharitable surmises, and slanderous
reports, which have with great vehemencie been blown
against vs.'[11] But the irate bishops were not to be appeased
by this means either. The people of Field's parish then
presented two petitions for 'the enlargement of their valuable
pastor, and learned and faithful preacher,' and some friends
used their influence, but Field and Wilcox remained in
prison. The prisoners next sought the aid of Leicester in
securing their release, sent a petition to the Lords of the
Council, and had a third petition sent in the names of their
wives and children. They complained at the length of their
imprisonment, the impoverishment of their families, the
unwholesome condition of the prison, the cold weather and
their impaired health. In spite of all their efforts, however, they were left to suffer the extreme penalty for their
offense. When they finally did secure their freedom, they,
together with some of the other leading Puritans, founded
the first Presbyterian church in England, at Wandsworth,
four miles from London.[12] Since the Commissioners were

---

[10] Daniel Neal, *History of the Puritans* (New York, 1856) I. 123.
For the account of Field's difficulties with the church I follow Neal
unless otherwise cited.

[11] J. Field and T. Wilcox, *A Confession of Faith*, in *Parte of a
Register*, p. 528.

[12] D. Lysons, *Environs of London* (London, 1810) I. 383.

unable to find out the names of the members of this presbytery, they summoned the heads of the Puritans to appear before the Ecclesiastical Commission to answer certain doctrinal questions. Field, Wilcox, and two others, being unable to answer satisfactorily, were sent forthwith to Newgate. We do not know how long this second period of imprisonment lasted. In a letter written by Field to Leicester in November, 1581, he speaks as if his release were a fairly recent thing.[13] In 1584 John Field admitted an 'unlawful conventicle' of ministers to his house and was suspended from the ministry.

Though Field was among the more than five hundred Puritan ministers who finally subscribed to the revised Discipline in 1586, his spirit had not been tamed. He collected many stories of ecclesiastical abuses and put them away in his study, in preparation for the time when another attempt might be made to apply the 'corrosive.' Upon his deathbed, Field 'willed they should be burnt and repented for collecting them,'[14] but his wish was not carried out. It was his material which appeared eight months later as the first of the Martin Marprelate tracts. If Field's dying wish had been fulfilled, the material for an expression of hatred toward the bishops would not have been at hand. Who can tell whether or not the controversy would even have materialized?

March 26, 1588, is an important date for stage-history. On that day John Field, the ardent Puritan minister of St. Giles, Cripplegate, and father of Nathan, was buried.[15] Had he lived to shape the character and form the ideals of the infant son that he left, one more ministerial voice might have been lifted up in Blackfriars, but the stage would have lost one of its best actors and most interesting minor writers.

[13] *MS. Cotton,* Titus B VII. fol. 22, British Museum.

[14] Edward Arber, *Introductory Sketch to the Marprelate Controversy* (London, 1879), p. 94.

[15] *Parish registers,* St. Giles, Cripplegate, London (burials, 1587-8).

John Field would never have allowed a son of his to cast a wishful eye toward a theatre, or to send so much as a truant thought down that primrose path, for he regarded players as 'evill men,' and plays as 'the schooles of as greate wickednesses as can be.'[16]   He exhorted even Lord Leicester to 'joyne with them that have longe, out of the word, cryed out against them:' and said, 'I am persuaded that if your honor knewe what sincks of synne they are, you would never looke once toward them.'   Nothing shows Field's utter lack of humor so well as that he could imagine Leicester's passing the theatre with averted eyes!   Field points out that Leicester's aid in behalf of the players had been a source of 'great griefe of all the godly,' and it is evident that no undue modesty prevents him from including himself among the aggrieved.   The Paris Garden disaster afforded Field an excellent opportunity to lift up his voice, and cry out against the theatre.   Four days after the accident, John Fleetwood, the Recorder, wrote Lord Burleigh: 'Vpon the same daye (i. e. Sunday, Jan. 13, 1583), the violators of the Sabothe were punished by God's providens at Paris garden and as I was writing of these last words loo here is a booke sette downe vpon the same matter.'[17]   With all the zeal of a reclaimer of the lost, Field had produced the little volume with the imposing title, 'God's Judgment shewed at Paris Garden, 13th January, 1583, being the Sabbath day at Beare Bayting, at the meeting of above 1000 persons, whereof divers were slayne, most maymed and hurt; set out with an exhortation for the observation of the Sabbath.' The gallery, he said, was 'strangely wrunge in peeces as it

[16] *MS. Cotton,* Titus B. VII. fol. 22, British Museum.   Letter to Lord Leicester, quoted in part by Collier, *English Dramatic Poetry and Annals of the Stage* (London, 1879) 1. 245.
[17] *Malone Society Collections* 1. 161.   Cf. 1. 64-6, letter of the Lord Mayor to the Privy Council.

were by God himself.' His sonorous sentences must have chilled the hearts of all who read: 'Beeing thvs vngodly assembled, to so vngodly a spectacle, and specially considering the time: the yeard, standings, and Galleries being ful fraught, being now amidst their iolity, when the dogs and Beare were in the chiefest battel, Lo, the mighty hand of God vpon them.'[18] By a queer twist of circumstance, it was John Field's son that drew the crowd back to this very spot some thirty years later, when the new Hope Theatre occupied the old Paris Garden site.

When John Field died, he left seven children, of whom the eldest was only seventeen. He left all his property to his wife, Joan, whom he made 'sole and onely executrix' of his will, trusting in 'her uprighte and motherly care of my children and hers and Christian disposition to deale towards all my creditors.'[19] Fortunately, the baptismal entries of all these children are preserved in the registers of St. Giles, Cripplegate.[20] The first child was a daughter, Dorcas, baptized May 7, 1570. The first son was baptized January 4, 1572, and was named for his father. Theophilus was baptized January 22, 1574; Jonathan, May 13, 1577; Nathaniel, June 13, 1581; Elizabeth, February 2, 1583; and Nathan, October 17, 1587. We know very little of the two daughters: Dorcas was married to Edward Rice on the ninth of November, 1590;[21] Elizabeth was buried at St. Anne, Blackfriars, on June 14, 1603,[22] when she had just reached twenty, the age at which Dorcas married. We know nothing of the life of John Field, junior. Jonathan Field, who died

---

[18] Quoted in *Notes and Queries* 4. 12 (1873), p. 312.

[19] Unpublished *will of John Field,* 38 Rutland. P.C.C.

[20] These entries are quoted by Collier, *op. cit.* 3. 425.

[21] *Parish register,* St. Giles, Cripplegate (marriages 1590). Cf. Collier, *op. cit.* 3. 426, note.

[22] *Parish register,* St. Anne, Blackfriars (burials, 1603), at St. Andrews-by-the-Wardrobe.

in 1640, wrote the epitaph inscribed under the bust of his brother, the Bishop of Hereford, in Hereford Cathedral. These verses are signed: 'Fratri moerenti moerens moriturus. Jonathan Field, Aet. LXII. MDCXL. Obiit.'[23]

Theophilus followed his father's profession. While, no doubt, John Field would have rejoiced to know that a son of his had entered the ministry, he would have grieved almost as much to see Theophilus a bishop as to see Nathan a player. In his forty-sixth year, Theophilus had reached the bishopric so bitterly denounced by his father, and it is to be feared that he climbed to the coveted goal by ways devious and none too pious. He was, however, a man of ability, and had received good training. He was a Cambridge M.A., and was elected Fellow of Pembroke Hall, October 9, 1598.[24] He was incorporated at Oxford July 16, 1600,[25] and later became B.D. and D.D. But preferment was to be secured not so much by worth as by political influence, and the ambitious Theophilus did not hesitate to use the latter as a means for advancement. Before 1609 he had become Chaplain to King James.[26] Later he was also appointed Chaplain to the Lord Chancellor Bacon.[27] After holding several vicarages, he was appointed Bishop of Llandaff on September 25, 1619,[28] by means of the influence of Buckingham.[29] In 1621 he was prosecuted for being

---

[23] Browne, Willis, *Survey of Cathedrals* (London, 1742) 2. 527.

[24] Foster, *op. cit.* 2. 490.

[25] Wood, *op. cit.* 1. 288.

[26] W. H. and H. C. Overall, *Analytical Index to the Remembrancia* (London, 1878), p. 131.

[27] *Calendar State Papers, Domestic Series, James I, 1619-23*, ed. Lemon and Green (London, 1858), p. 238.

[28] Le Neve, *Fasti Ecclesiæ Anglicanæ* (Oxford, 1854) 2. 253. Cf. T. Birch, *The Court and Times of James I* (London, 1848) 2. 167. Rev. Thomas Larkin writes to Sir Thomas Puckering, May 24, 1619: 'Dr. Field, (Field, the player's brother), shall succeed Llandaff.'

[29] J. Harington, *Nugæ Antiquæ* (London, 1804) 2. 222.

involved, before his promotion, in one of the largest bribes offered to Bacon. Carte reports that the Upper House 'cleared the bishop of the charge of bribery, but as it was not a fitting thing for a clergyman to be concerned in a brocage of such nature, the house required the archbishop of Canterbury to give him an admonition as doctor Field, not as Bishop of Llandaff, in the convocation house, which was done accordingly.'[30]

Since the position as Bishop of Llandaff did not satisfy Theophilus, he interceded with Buckingham to get him a better position. He also tactfully tried to interest the King in his behalf. In 1624 he presented the King with a sermon called 'The Earth's Encrease; or a Communion Cup,' instead of presenting the cup itself, which was the customary New Year's gift of the Court Chaplain to the King. He explained the substitution on the grounds of poverty. But Buckingham was not forgotten even in this scheme, for the third dedication of this sermon was to Buckingham! His attitude toward Buckingham was always one of fulsome flattery. He wrote him in 1626: 'In the great librarie of men, that I have studied these many yeeres, your Grace is the best booke, and most classick author, that I have read: in whome I fynde so much goodnes, sweetnes, and noblenes of nature; such an heroick spirit, so boundlesse bounty, as I never did in any.'[31] He reminded Buckingham that 'none that ever looked toward your Grace, did ever goe emptie away,' and told him 'one blast of your breath is able to bring me to the haven where I would be.' In 1627 Theophilus was promoted by Buckingham's influence to the bishopric of St. David's, but St. David's was not the appointment that he desired. Furthermore, his health was so poor there that he returned to Gloucester to live. In spite of his continuous flattery of Buckingham, it was not until December 15,

---

[30] T. Carte, *A General History of England* (London, 1750) 4. 77.

[31] Harington, *op. cit.* 2. 122-3.

1635,[32] that Theophilus was appointed Bishop of Hereford. Though his translation was hurried through, his health had become so impaired that he did not live long to enjoy his preferment. He died June 2, 1636, and was buried in Hereford Cathedral. Below his bust is the Latin epitaph composed by his brother, and a word-play in English on Field:[33]

> Aspicis effigiem Cleri par nulla figura
> Theophili genio; qui fuit orbis honos
> Doctior an melior fuit haud scio. Fama docebit,
> Quod si fama negat, tu pia scripta lege
> Lux Landavensis, Menevensis, et Herefordensis
> Haud Sterili tumulo clauditur almus Ager
> Praesulis officio functus qui triplicis olim
> Hic jacet hic toto flumine flendus Ager
> Qualis odor variis distincti floribus Agri
> Non minus est grati noster odoris Ager.

> *Anagram, He Faild Not Any*

> The sun that Light unto three Churches gave,
> Is set. The Field is buried in a Grave.
> This Sun shall rise, this Field renew his Flowers;
> This Sweetness breathe for Ages, not for Howers.

His will, leaving all his possessions to his wife, Alice, is preserved in Somerset House, London.[34] That he had accumulated a good deal of property is shown by the will of his wife, which lists considerable holdings in the parish of St. Clement Danes (including Nags Head Tavern), and the 'Castle and Manor of Penhon in the County of Monmouth together with all the lands and Tenements, leases, Rents, services, and appurtanences.'[35]

In spite of the fact that the parish registers of St. Giles, Cripplegate, record a *Nathaniell Feilde*, 1581, and a *Nathan*

---

[32] Le Neve, *op. cit.* 1. 471.
[33] Willis, *op. cit.* 2. 526-7.
[34] 82 *Pile,* P.C.C.
[35] 7 *Goare,* P.C.C.

Feilde, 1587, both sons of the minister, John Field, the similarity of the name has led to the confusion of the identity of Nathaniel, the printer, and Nathan, the actor-playwright. It was assumed that John Field could not have had two living sons with these names. That this assumption was based upon insufficient evidence, is shown by the fact that in naming his sons Nathan and Nathaniel, John Field was only completing an odd quartette begun with John, 1572, and Jonathan, 1577. John and Jonathan seem to have preserved distinct identities, but Nathan and Nathaniel became almost hopelessly confused.

The history of this confusion of names is an interesting one. The first time that the name Nathaniel occurs in connection with the actor is in two of the six lists of actors recorded in the 1679 folio of the Beaumont-Fletcher plays. Here, in the lists of *The Loyal Subject* and *The Mad Lover,* the name is given *Nathanaell.* Before this time all the formal documents referring to the actor give the name *Nathan.* In the account of his impressment for the Chapel Royal[36] the name is *Nathan ffeilde.* The agreement with Henslowe and Meade in regard to the Hope Theatre is made by *Nathan ffeilde gent.*[37] The name appears as Nathan in Cunningham's record of the payment for the court performance of *Bartholomew Fair,* November 1, 1614;[38] in the Patent for the King's Men, March 27, 1619;[39] in the Livery Allowance, May 19, 1619;[40] in the documents of the Witter-Hemings case where reference is

[36] F. G. Fleay, *Chronicle History of the London Stage* (London, 1890) 1. 128.

[37] *Henslowe Papers,* ed. Greg (London, 1907), p. 23.

[38] Peter Cunningham, *Extracts from the Accounts of the Revels at the Court in the Reign of Queen Elizabeth and King James I* (Printed for the Shakespeare Soc., London, 1842), p. xliv.

[39] *The English Drama and the Stage,* ed. W. C. Hazlitt (Printed for the Roxburghe Library, London, 1869), pp. 50-2.

[40] *Report of the Historical Manuscripts Commission* (London, 1874) 4. 299.

made to his share in the Globe; [41] in the 1623 folio of Shakespeare's plays; in the entry in the *Stationers' Register* of the collaborative play, *The Jeweler of Amsterdam;* [42] and below his portrait in Dulwich College. In other contemporary documents the name is found in abbreviated form, never as Nathaniel. The actor-lists of the Jonson plays give *Nat.;* Field's early commendatory verses are signed *Nat., Nath.,* or *N. F.;* Chapman's verses are addressed to *Nat Field;* and Field's letters to Henslowe are signed *Nat.* Yet in the face of the above evidence, every early biographer, beginning with Langbaine in *Momus Triumphans* (1688), gives the name of the player as Nathaniel. Until recently these biographers have been followed in this error by even the most reputable scholars. The first person to suspect the confusion of names was Joseph Hunter. In the manuscript biographical sketches, *Chorus Vatum,* [43] Hunter calls Field the player 'a wild irregular person,' and tries to get around identifying him as the son of the Puritan minister. He says, however, 'If it should ever turn out that Field the actor was son of John Field the divine I should think that the entry of the apprenticeship belongs to Nathaniel the son born 1581, and that it was Nathan, born 1587 who was the actor.' William Rendle in his book, *Old Southwark and Its People* (London, 1878, p. 175), correctly refers to the player as Nathan. Just as I am completing this monograph, Mr. Chambers has published his conclusion based on the actor's signatures, that Nathan and Nathaniel were distinct individuals. [44] Mr. Chambers does not, however, have the

---

[41] C. W. Wallace, *Shakespeare and His London Associates, Univ. of Neb. St.* 10. 63 (1910).

[42] Eyre and Rivington, *Transcript of the Stationers' Register* (London, 1913) 1. 445.

[43] J. Hunter, *Chorus Vatum Anglicanorum,* Add. MSS. Brit. Mus. 24490.

[44] E. K. Chambers, *Elizabethan Stage* (London, 1923) 2. 316-8.

final evidence presented below that both Nathaniel and Nathan lived to maturity, and carried on separate professions in the same general locality in London.

Instead of questioning this matter of dual personality, biographers who have been aware of the two baptismal entries have gone to various lengths in accounting for the similarity of name. Collier, for example, assumed that Nathaniel died in infancy, since a second son was named Nathan. He did not, however, suggest the death of John to account for Jonathan! He ignored the fact that there is no record of any such death in the parish registers of St. Giles, Cripplegate, though these registers contain an unusually complete account of the Field family. Various biographers have overlooked the inconsistency of attributing the printer's apprenticeship of Nathaniel to Nathan when Nathan was not even nine years old, and was probably then attending St. Paul's Grammar School, in which he was a scholar when he was impressed for the Chapel Royal in 1600.

How did this vexing problem of Nathan versus Nathaniel originate? Was it due to the two actor-lists of the Beaumont-Fletcher folio, or had the names been confused earlier? Some basis for the interchange, it seems to me, extends as far back as the baptismal records of the parish of St. Anne, Blackfriars, 1619-27. The first two entries of the children of Nathaniel and Anne Field give the name of the father as Nathan, but the appearance of the entry indicates abbreviation. One of these entries is corrected in the register; when the second child died, the record of his burial gives him as the son of Nathaniel and Anne Field.[45] Collier seems not to have noted this fact, and even Mr. Chambers assumes that children of both Nathan and Nathaniel are given in these registers.[46]

[45] Cf. *baptisms,* Jan. 12, 1620, and *burials,* Feb. 2, 1623 (Theophilus Field).

[46] Chambers, *op. cit.* 2. 317.

The separate identity of the brothers is definitely proved by two letters of administration which I found among the documents of Somerset House. The first and most important of these is the grant of letters of administration to Dorcas, the oldest child of John Field and wife of Edward Rice, giving her the administration of the goods of her brother, Nathan Field.[47] The second is the commission granted on March 26, 1632 (1633), to Anne Field for the administration of the goods of her husband, Nathaniel.[48]

Relatively little is known about Nathaniel. He was the fifth child of John Field, and was born on 13 June, 1581, when the Field family was undergoing many vicissitudes. His father was either then in Newgate, or had been recently released by the intervention of Leicester. In 1596 he was apprenticed to Ralph Jackson, Stationer, of London.[49] Though the entry names the period of apprenticeship as eight years, Nathaniel did not take up his freedom until 1611.[50] He seems to have found difficulty in entering his profession, for it is not until 1624 that the *Stationers' Register* records the license of a book for Nathaniel Field. Field is associated with Thomas Harper, who also took up his freedom in 1611 (Arber 3.29). Between the years 1624 and 1628 five sermons by Theophilus Field, Nathaniel's brother, are licensed to Nathaniel Field and Thomas Harper (Arber 4.133, 137, 167, 191). The last entry to Nathaniel Field is November 9, 1627 (Arber 4.188). This is the entry of the book called *The true historye of the tragique loves of Hipolito and Isabella,* which is interesting because it contains verses by Chapman, the friend of Nathan. In 1629, however, Harper published Chapman's *Justification of Nero*

[47] *Admon. Act Book,* 1620, P.C.C.
[48] *Probate and Admon. Act Book,* 1632, P.C.C.
[49] E. Arber, *Transcript of the Stationers' Register, 1544-1640* (London, 1875-7) 2. 215.
[50] *Ibid.* 2. 215 and 3. 683.

alone. Between the years 1619 and 1627 the parish registers of St. Anne, Blackfriars, record the birth of five children, and the burial of two in infancy. They also register the burial of Nathaniel on February 20, 1632-3. On March 26 letters of administration were granted to his wife:

On the 26th day of March 1632 Letters of Administration were granted to Anne Feild relict of Nathaniel Feild late of the parish of Saint Anne Blackfryers London intestate deceased to administer the goods credits chattels etc. of the said deceased etc.

These goods were appraised at £45, 14s, 11d. His wife seems to have survived him several years, for she is found among the witnesses of the will of Alice Field, wife of Theophilus, in 1636.[51]

Our knowledge of the life of the actor, Nathan, is largely restricted to his connection with dramatic companies. He was attending 'Mr. Monkaster's school' (St. Paul's, 1596-1608) when he was seized for the Chapel Royal in 1600 by the authority of the Queen's commission to Nathaniel Giles.[52] If Nathan entered school at the usual age for beginning grammar school at that time, he would have had four years in school before his impressment. His seizure marks his departure from the Puritan influences of his home, and his entry upon a dramatic career.

Although Nathan's profession was an innovation in the Field family, and he was probably thought of as the black sheep that had broken all the family traditions, he carried with him into this new sphere of life many of the family traits. The Fields were a well-educated, scholarly people, from whom Nathan seems to have inherited the desire to be learned. Even though only a child of thirteen years, he pored over his Latin during the time in which the other Chapel children were probably playing. He was sufficiently

[51] 7 *Goare,* P.C.C.
[52] Fleay, *op. cit.* I. 128.

earnest to attract the attention and aid of Ben Jonson. He
seems to have possessed those characteristics which made the
Fields successful men. Like his father, he endeared himself to his associates. This was such a noticeable trait that
all his early biographers make an especial point of the fact
that he was 'greatly esteem'd' by his contemporaries. He
had a bright and attractive personality that could win men
as different in nature as Jonson, Burbadge, and Henslowe.
He was tactful in his management of men, and knew how
to mingle judicious flattery, pointed argument, and a wise
self-appreciation, so that he was able to overcome opposition.
He was as quick to detect hypocrisy as was John Field,
and as fearless in revealing it. John Field had seen the
hypocrisy which had resulted from the substitution of the
forms and ceremonies of religion for the spirit itself;
Nathan saw that the very Puritanism which his father had
thought to be a remedy for the situation had come to be
merely a pious mask behind which immorality dwelt.
Fundamentally, both the Puritan divine and the playwright
who satirized Puritans were fighting the whited sepulchre
full of dead men's bones. Although as a player and an
author of plays, Nathan would have been considered a very
wicked man by his father, he kept somewhat of the family
piety even within the 'synckes of sinne' themselves. He
always mentions the name of God in a reverent way. In
Woman is a Weathercock, for example, he shows one of the
characters trusting in God to aid in righting a wrong that
had been done to her; in Act IV he is quite serious in
pointing out God's just distribution of wealth and wisdom.
In a letter written in 1616, defending his profession, he says
that he has studied the Bible as his 'best parte,' and he
professes: 'I love the Sanctuary of my God and worship
towardes his holy altar.'[53] He says that he has endeavored

[53] J. O. Halliwell-Phillipps, *Illustrations of the Life of Shakespeare*
(London, 1874), pp. 115-6.

'to make sure' his election, and calls upon his conscience to witness: 'I beare in my soul the badge of a Christian practise to live the lief of the faithfull, wish to dye the death of the righteous, and hope to meete my Saviour in the cloudes.' Surely this is an echo of the same spirit which dwelt in the hearts of the many divines in the Field connection.

CHAPTER II

FIELD'S CONNECTION WITH DRAMATIC COMPANIES

Field's induction into a dramatic career came very unexpectedly when he was about thirteen years old. One day as he was on his way to Mulcaster's school (St. Paul's), he was 'taken up' by James Robinson under the authority of the commission granted to Nathaniel Giles in 1597 for impressing children for the Chapel Royal.[1] In its wording Giles's Commission covered the taking up of children for singing only, but the interpretation was broader than that. In the time of Edwards and of Hunnis, the earlier masters of the Children of the Chapel Royal, at least a part of the children had been trained as actors for the entertainment of their play-loving Queen. Giles, as Master of the Chapel Royal, was not required to instruct more than twelve children for the Chapel Royal, but his Commission did not limit the number he might take up under the Queen's authority, and did not restrict his employment of them. He was even granted money to pay for 'the conveyance of the said Children from any place' and for lodging 'when they for our service shall remove to any place or places.' From the complaint of Henry Clifton in regard to the impressment of his son,[2] we learn that Giles, Henry Evans, James Robinson, and others interpreted this Commission in such a way as to enable them to raise a company of boy-actors which they established at Blackfriars. During the year that elapsed between the impressment of Thomas Clifton and the Court Proceedings in regard to the case, the irate Henry Clifton collected information in regard to other boys who had been kidnapped in like manner, and presented a list of seven

[1] Wallace, *Children of the Chapel at Blackfriars, Un. of Neb. Studies* 8. 61 (1908).
[2] Fleay, *Stage,* pp. 127-32.

names. Third in this list is the name of 'Nathan ffield, a scholler of a gramer schole in London, kepte by one M^r. Monkaster.' Clifton said that these boys were not taken for the Chapel Royal, but were employed 'only in playes and interludes.'

This document throws interesting light on the method of impressment used by Giles's deputy, Robinson, and enables us to picture the similar occurrence on the day that Field was seized. Clifton's son was also thirteen years old and a grammar school student. As he was 'walking quietly from your subiect's sayd howse towards the sayd schole,' says Clifton, James Robinson waylaid him and 'wth greate force & vyolence did seise & surprise, & him wth lyke force & vyolence did, to the greate terror & hurte of him the sayd Thomas Clifton, hall, pull, dragge, and carrye awaye to the said playe howse in the black fryers aforesayd, threatening him that yf he, the said Thomas Clifton, would not obey him, the sayd Robinson, that he, the sayd Robinson, would chardge the counstable wth him the sayd Thomas Clifton.'[3] Thomas Clifton was then 'comitted to the said playe howse amongste a companie of lewd & dissolute mercenary players,' given a part of a play to learn the same 'by harte,' put into the custody of Evans, and threatened with a whipping if he did not obey. Giles, Evans, and Robinson 'vtterly & scornfully refused' to release Thomas Clifton to his father, and so Henry Clifton appealed to Sir John Fortescue, a member of the Privy Council, by whose influence the 'sayd son' was set at liberty. Field did not have a father and influential friends to take his part; so with the fear of a whipping hanging over him, he probably learned the lines assigned to him and without more ado settled down into life at the Blackfriars.

On September 2, 1600, preceding the seizures mentioned in Clifton's complaint, Henry Evans had leased the Black-

---

[3] *Ibid.*, p. 129.

friars building from Richard Burbadge for twenty-one years.[4] Without changing the roof and building twelve rooms above the 'Great Hall' as Mr. Wallace does,[5] we are able to find lodging for the boy-actors within the Blackfriars. From the deed of sale to Burbadge,[6] we learn that the old Parliament Chamber above the great hall had already been divided into seven rooms and, since it had a separate stairway, was being used as an apartment. The deed of sale speaks of this part of the building as 'all those seven great upper rooms as they are now divided, being all upon one floor, and sometime being one great and entire room.' Mr. Adams suggests[7] that this apartment was kept as a lodging for the boy-actors.

Mr. Wallace has shown that between twenty and twenty-five boys were required in the production of some of the plays of the Blackfriars repertory.[8] In the lawsuit, *Keysar versus Burbadge,*[9] Keysar states that the company of the Children's Revels numbered eighteen or twenty, 1608-10, though the Burbadges deny that the company is so large. In this connection it is interesting to note that the confirmation in 1623 of the 1617 license for the Children of the Queen's Revels states that the company shall not exceed twenty in number. Chambers[10] does not think that two distinct sets of children were maintained, one for the Chapel Royal and one for plays, but believes that the choir boys were utilized in the stage performances, especially when there was music in the play. The renewal of Giles's Com-

[4] *Ibid.* (Evans versus Kirkham), pp. 211 and 230.
[5] Wallace, *op. cit.,* pp. 40-1.
[6] Halliwell-Phillipps, *Outlines of the Life of Shakespeare* (London, 1887) I. 229. Cf. *Malone Soc. Col.* 2. 60 and 70.
[7] J. Q. Adams, *Shakespearean Playhouses* (Cambridge, 1917), p. 192.
[8] Wallace, *op. cit.,* pp. 74-5.
[9] Wallace, *Shakespeare and His London Associates, Univ. of Neb. St.* 10. 90 (1910).
[10] Chambers, *op. cit.* 2. 48.

mission in 1606 is further evidence that the Children of the
Chapel Royal had formerly taken part in the plays, for it
states that the impressed children are not to become players,
'for that it is not fitt or decent that such as shoulde singe
the praises of God Allmightie shoulde be trayned vpp or
imployed in suche lascivious and prophane exercises.'[11]
We know the names of eleven of the boys with whom
Field was associated at this time. These are: John Chapel,
John Motteram, Alvery Trussell, Philip Pykman, Thomas
Grimes, Salathiel Pavy (Clifton's complaint); Thomas
Day, John Underwood, Robert Baxter, John Frost (actor-
list of *Cynthia's Revels*); William Ostler, and Thomas
Morton (actor-list of *Poetaster*). No doubt these boys were
very congenial. Field, Chapel, and Motteram had in com-
mon the background of grammar school life. The boys
were about the same age: in 1600 Field was just thirteen;
Clifton states that his son was 'about the age of thirteen
years;' and Jonson's *Epitaph on Salathiel Pavy* gives Pavy's
age as 'scarce thirteen.' Pavy, Trussell, Pykman, and
Grimes were all apprentices when Robinson took them for
the Queen's service, and were probably about the same age.
The children selected were of unusual ability. Clifton
reports that Robinson and his confederates impressed those
children 'whome they thought moste fittest to acte and
furnish the said playes.' Jonson's epitaph shows that at
least they had not overestimated Pavy's ability.

The boy-actors were placed in the Blackfriars under the
supervision of Evans and were lodged, fed, and educated,
as well as taught to act in plays. The Duke of Stettin-
Pomerania, who visited the Blackfriars Theatre in 1602,
seems to have been especially impressed by the good education given the boy-actors. He says, 'The origin of this
Children's Comœdiam is this: the Queen keeps a number
of young boys who have to apply themselves zealously to

[11] *Malone Society Collections* I. 362.

the art of singing and to learn all the various musical instruments, and to pursue their studies at the same time.   These boys have special præceptores in all the different arts, especially very good musicos.'[12]   We know that Latin was one of Field's subjects, for Drummond quotes Jonson as saying, 'Nid Field was his schollar, and he had read to him the *Satyres of Horace* and some *Epigrames of Martiall*.'[13] There seems to have been ample time for the boys to acquire an education in addition to learning to perform plays, for the full time for the production of plays was only six months in the year,[14] and according to the Duke of Stettin-Pomerania, the boys were required to act a play only once a week.

The relation between the young actors and their poets was a very friendly one.   The gentler side of Jonson's nature is revealed when he takes time to help the boy Field with his lessons, and when he pours out his sense of personal loss in the *Epitaph on Salathiel Pavy,* the tenderest piece of writing that he ever did.   Jonson's friendship for Field was more than that of patron for protégé.   In the Elizabethan period the difference of approximately a decade and a half in age made a very real barrier, but by his own merit Field was able to surmount this and become a contributor as well as receiver in the friendship between them.   Field's attitude of hero-worship is shown in the verses prefixed to *Volpone.* Here he addresses Jonson as 'worthiest Maister,' and says that it is 'damnable presumption' on his part to dare to commend Jonson or the play.   When Jonson produced *Catiline* in 1611, Field again wrote verses addressed to his 'worthy and beloved friend.'   In Field's verses commending Fletcher's

[12] *Diary of the Duke of Stettin's Journey, Transactions of the Royal Historical Society,* New Series 6. 27 (1892).

[13] W. Drummond, *Conversations,* ed. Laing (Printed for the Shakespeare Society, London, 1842), p. 11.

[14] H. N. Hillebrand, *Child Actors, Univ. of Ill. Studies* 11. 335 (1926).

The Faithful Shepherdess, there is indication of a warm personal relationship between the two young poets, for Field addresses Fletcher as 'loved friend' and alludes to some private conversation in which he had discussed his own dramatic aspirations with Fletcher. The older playwright, Chapman, was also attracted by Field and calls him 'loved son' in an encouraging letter of commendation prefixed to Field's first play, *Woman is a Weathercock*.

The association with the poets was not, however, always pleasant. Some insight into the experiences of these children is given in the *Induction* to *Cynthia's Revels*. When Jonson is asked for, the second child says: 'We are not so officiously befriended by him as to have his presence in the tiring house to prompt us aloud, stamp at the book-holder, swear for our properties, curse the poor tireman, rail the music out of tune, and sweat for every venial trespass we commit, as another author would, if he had such fine enghles as we.'

To us of the twentieth century, there is something pitiful in the use of the asseveration, 'Would I were whipped,' by these boy-actors. It seems that Evans attempted to avoid spoiling the child by following the ancient precept. When Thomas Clifton was impressed, he was told that 'yf he did not obey the sayd Evans, he should be surely whipped.' In the prologue to the *Second Part of the Return from Parnassus*, there is a little incident which might well have taken place in the Blackfriars. The boy begins the prologue, but forgets. The stage-keeper threatens him, 'You would be whipt, you raskall: you must be sitting up all night at cardes when you should be conning your part.' The boy explains that his failure is the stage-keeper's fault: 'It's all long of you, I could not get my part a night or two before, that I might sleepe on it.' The angry stage-keeper then 'carrieth the boy away under his arme,' and the sequel may be inferred. Robert Armin attributes the good acting done by the Children to this method of securing results: 'Such was the cinnicke, onskilfull in quips and worldly flaunts,

rather *to play with short rods, and give venies till all smarte
againe;* not in the braines as the World did, but *in the
buttocks, as such doe, having their joses displaied making
them expert till they cry it up in the top of the question.*[15]

The Children of the Queen's Revels were not boasting
when they called themselves 'fine enghles.' In its earlier
years the company was looked upon as a serious rival of the
men's companies. Shakespeare acknowledged its popularity,
and in the famous Hamlet passage on the 'little eyases' passed
his half-humorous judgment on such a company. His only
criticism of the company was that the playwrights were setting the boys in opposition to the adult companies, which
most of them would later join. When Johannes Rhenanus
visited England, he called the Children's company 'die best
Compagnia in Lunden.'[16] Robert Keysar, who became
manager of the company, described it as 'a company of the
most exparte and skillfull acto[rs] w[th]in the Realme of England.'[17] The Children had made such a reputation for
themselves even as early as 1601 that they were brought to
Court on Twelfth Night and Shrove Sunday to play before
the Queen.[18] This was the first appearance of the Children
at Court since 1584. Field's ability is shown by the fact
that he was the leading actor for such a company as this.

Clifton's Complaint, brought before the Star Chamber
in December, 1601, and acted upon early in 1602, resulted
in a change of management for the Children at Blackfriars.
On account of his abuse of the Queen's Commission for
impressing boys, Evans was forced to 'avoyd and leave the
country.' He turned over his interests to his son-in-law,

[15] R. Armin, *Nest of Ninnies*, Shakespeare Society Publications 10.
55 (1842).

[16] *Itinerarium der Reise von Cassel aus in Engelandt, A. 1611*, Bibl.
Cass. Mscr. Hass. 4. 66, fol. 80-168, quoted in part by Philip Losch in
his monograph on Johannes Rhenanus (Marburg, 1895).

[17] Wallace, *op. cit.,* p. 90.

[18] Cunningham, *op. cit.*, p. xxxiii.

Alexander Hawkins, who, in partnership with Edward Kirkham, Thomas Kendall, and Robert Payne, continued the
company. We can imagine the excitement that the enforced
departure of Evans and the installation of a new system of
management created among these boy-actors still in their
early teens.

The theatres were closed a great deal in 1603, first, on
account of the Queen's death, March 24, and later, because
of the severity of the plague, which compelled the theatres
to remain closed from about May on through the year.
The boys must have wondered what the future held for them,
for Evans was even then negotiating with Burbadge in
regard to giving up the Blackfriars lease.[19]

February 4, 1604, Kirkham, Hawkins, Kendall, and Payne
secured a patent from James I for the Children at Blackfriars.[20] The Queen took the company under her patronage
and allowed them the title of 'Children of the Revels to the
Queen.' Samuel Daniel was given the censorship of plays
for the company. Although the plague had not abated sufficiently for the theatres to open before April, 1604,[21] the
Children acted before the Court in February.[22] Once more
Field was in the presence of royalty, this time displaying
his powers before the new King.

The year 1604 began an exciting and troubled career for
the Children of the Queen's Revels. When the theatres
were opened in the spring, the Children acted Daniel's play,
Philotas. Since this play was thought to relate to the Earl
of Essex, it met with severe disapproval. By January, 1605,
however, the Children had been taken back into favor and
were allowed to present two plays at Court.[23] The payment
for both performances was made to Evans and Daniel; so

[19] Fleay, *op. cit.*, p. 235.
[20] *Malone Society Collections* 1. 267-8.
[21] J. T. Murray, *English Dramatic Companies* (London, 1910) 1. 354.
[22] Cunningham, *op. cit.*, p. xxxvii.
[23] *Ibid.*, p. xxxvi.

it seems that Evans was again recognized in connection with the company. The Children and Samuel Daniel had not learned prudence from their experience with *Philotas* and in 1605 produced *Eastward Hoe,* the collaborative work of Jonson, Chapman, and Marston, in which the authors dared to ridicule not only the Scots but also the King himself. This brought serious trouble. The company was deprived of the patronage of the Queen and inhibited from acting. Kirkman withdrew from the management of the company, and two of the authors and some of the actors were imprisoned.[24] Since Field was the leading actor, we may safely assume that at the age of seventeen he was experiencing life in an Elizabethan prison, in company with his older friends, Jonson and Chapman. On account of this trouble Evans made another attempt to give up the lease of Blackfriars, but was again unsuccessful.

Meantime the Blackfriars Children did not profit by experience, and in February, 1606, when allowed the performance of Day's *Isle of Gulls,* the company was once more in trouble for offending the Court. Again 'sundry' were committed to prison, this time to Bridewell.[25] Field was, doubtless, among the 'sundry.'

The theatre could not have been closed for long, for early in 1608 the company was not only playing but had sufficiently forgotten its former troubles to ridicule the nobility again on the stage. There seems to have been a series of offences. One of these was on account of a scene in a play not now extant, but referred to by the French Ambassador, M. de la Boderie, in a letter to M. de Puiseux at Paris.[26] He wrote that the Children of the Revels had

[24] Murray, *op. cit.* 1. 355.

[25] T. Birch, *Court and Times of James the First* (London, 1848) 1. 60-1. Quoted by Chambers, 'Court Performances of James I,' *Modern Language Review* 4. 158 (1909).

[26] Le Fevre, de la Boderie, *Ambassade de Monsieur de la Boderie en Angleterre, 1606-11* (London, 1750) 3. 196. Quoted by Chambers, 'Court Performances under James I,' *Mod. Lang. Rev.* 4. 158 (1909).

dared to represent the English King in a comic scene. A short time after this the company acted Chapman's *Conspiracy and Tragedy of Charles, Duke of Byron*. Boderie was offended by the representation of the French Court in these plays and secured an order against their further presentation. This was ineffective, however, and the Children added to their former offenses by introducing the Queen and Madame Verneuil 'traitant celle-ci fort mal de paroles, et lui donnant un soufflet.' The Ambassador then complained to Salisbury, and the old danger of imprisonment was impending. Chapman succeeded in making his escape, but Boderie says that they found three of the actors, who were at once sent to prison. Was Field so unlucky as to be one of the three? The King was now so thoroughly annoyed that he ordered all the theatres closed. In July the plague broke out with such violence that the theatres were closed until December, 1609. From the lawsuit of *Evans versus Kirkham,* [27] we learn that about July 26, 1608, Kirkham had dissolved the Children of the Revels and divided the property. Evans considered his theatrical project finally ended, gave up his commission, and discharged the dramatists.[28] Once more the surrender of the lease of the Blackfriars was taken up with Burbadge, though it seems that the negotiations were not concluded until about August 10, 1609.[29]

We learn from the lawsuit of *Keysar v. Burbage* that the many misfortunes which had befallen the Blackfriars Children did not at once put an end to the company.[30] For a time Keysar maintained the Children at his own expense, thinking that the company might yet be successful on account of the number, training, and talent of the actors. In his *Bill of Complaint* (February 8, 1610) he says that he has

---

[27] Fleay, *op. cit.*, pp. 221.
[28] Fleay, *op. cit.*, p. 222.
[29] Wallace, *Shakespeare and His London Associates*, p. 87.
[30] *Ibid.*, pp. 80-97.

'kept boyes theise Two yeares to his exceedinge Charge of
purpose to have Continewed playes in the said howse vpon
the ceasing of the general sickness.'[31]   We know that they
were in his charge in December, 1608, and January, 1609.
The payment for two performances given by the 'children
of the blackfriers' at Court Christmas, 1608,[32] and for a
play presented by them on the fourth of January is made
to 'Roberte Keyser.'[33]   Where he lodged the company is
uncertain, but since the King's Men did not come over to
the Blackfriars Theatre until the final surrender of the
lease (August, 1609), it is conceivable that he remained
at Blackfriars.   The fact that the company was still termed
the Children of the Blackfriars in the above mentioned payments lends countenance to this view.[34]

The continuance of the plague and the cost of maintaining
the company finally discouraged Keysar; the company was
dispersed, and the players 'driven each of them to provide
for himselfe.'   The King's Men took over Underwood,
Ostler, and perhaps temporarily, Field,[35] though I am inclined
to think that the inclusion of Field's name at this time is a
mistake.

Sometime in 1609, probably in the fall, Keysar, Rosseter,
and other partners took over the lease of the Whitefriars
Theatre from Drayton and his company and established
there a company of boy-actors.[36]   The company, which is
now called the Children of the Whitefriars, appeared before
the Court five times during the winter of 1609-1610.   Field
returned to the company (if, indeed, he had joined the
King's Men in the fall of 1609), and before March, 1610,

[31] *Ibid.,* p. 83.
[32] Chambers, *op. cit.,* p. 154.
[33] Hillebrand, *op. cit.,* p. 201, note 65.
[34] Cf. Chambers, *Elizabethan Stage* 2. 55.
[35] Halliwell-Phillipps, *op. cit.* 1. 317.
[36] Hillebrand, 'Children of the King's Revels at Whitefriars,' *Jour.
of Eng. and Ger. Phil.* (1922), pp. 318-25.

was acting in the leading rôle in Jonson's *Epicoene*. Richard Baxter is the only one of Field's old associates whose name appears in the list of actors for this play. On January 4, 1610, a patent was granted to Robert Daborne, Philip Rosseter, John Tarbock, and Robert Browne, authorizing the Children of the Queen's Revels to play in the Whitefriars Theatre.[37] Though Keysar's name is not mentioned in the patent, the Keysar-Burbadge papers term Keysar a partner. The company remained under this organization in apparent prosperity until March, 1613, when Rosseter united companies with Henslowe. This company was very popular at Court and appeared before royalty sixteen times between 1604 and 1613.

In March, 1613, Rosseter incorporated the Children of the Queen's Revels with the Lady Elizabeth's men. The new company probably continued to act at Whitefriars for a time at least, for Rosseter had engaged the Whitefriars until December 25, 1614. Marston's *Insatiate Countess,* which was acted at the Whitefriars in 1613, must have been produced after the amalgamation of the two companies, since the name of William Barkstead, a member of the original Lady Elizabeth's company, appears on the title page. It is possible, however, that the new company also acted at the Swan. Henslowe seems to have established the Lady Elizabeth's men there, for the title page of Middleton's *Chaste Maid in Cheapside* states that it was acted by the Lady Elizabeth's men at the Swan. This theatre was in use continuously from 1611 to 1615, for the *Accounts of the Overseers of the Poor of Paris Garden*[38] show receipts from

---

[37] *Malone Society Collections* 1. 271-2. Collier forges a version of this license, giving patentees as 'Robert Daborne, Willm̃ Shakespeare, Nathaniel Field, and Edward Kirkham.'

[38] P. Norman, *The Accounts of the Overseers of the Poor of Paris Garden, Southwark, 17 May 1608 to 30 September 1617* (London, 1901). Cf. Wallace, 'The Swan Theatre,' *Englische Studien* 43. 390 (note 1).

the Swan, though the receipts for 1615 were so small that it appears that the theatre was used very little during that year. On August 29, 1613, Henslowe, in partnership with Jacob Meade, took steps to provide the company with a permanent theatre, modeled after the Swan, which was to be built on the site of the old Bear Garden.[39] By the terms of the contract, the carpenter was to complete the new theatre by the last day of November; but since it was September before he engaged a bricklayer,[40] it is unlikely that the building was completed by that date. Just when the company went over to the Bankside and occupied the Hope, as the new theatre was called, is uncertain, but the first play known to have been acted there is *Bartholomew Fair,* performed October 31, 1614. When Henslowe broke the company, March, 1614, Rosseter withdrew; the change in theatres probably occurred at this time.

The new company began under unfavorable conditions, and its history includes many vicissitudes. The first year was a losing struggle against indebtedness. The company was formed with an initial debt of £320 overhanging it. This debt was augmented by the fact that two members of the company borrowed £50 from Henslowe, and Henslowe, to insure repayment, added their private debt to the general account. Among other complaints set forth by the company in the *Articles of Grievance and Oppression,*[41] drawn up in 1615, is the accusation that during the first year Henslowe sold a part of the stock of apparel which he held as security for the debt, without 'accomptynge or abatinge for the same.' At the end of the year the company had not fully paid its debt to Henslowe, and so Henslowe broke the company and took over all the stock. This step on Henslowe's part brought about several changes. Ecclestone left the company. Rosseter gave up his connection with the players; and in

[39] Greg, *op. cit.,* p. 19.
[40] *Ibid.,* p. 22.
[41] Greg, *op. cit.,* p. 86.

March, 1614, when Henslowe made up his company anew, he sold a quantity of costumes to Henslowe. The warrants for Court performances, which had formerly been made out to Rosseter, were thereafter made out to Field. The company was reorganized; and Field, who held a place of importance in the company as leading actor and successful playwright, took over the business management of the company, representing its members in a new contract with Henslowe and Meade.[42]

It is impossible to assume that Prince Charles's company joined with that of Henslowe in March, 1614, for on May 18, 1614, the Prince's men were playing in Norwich.[43] The warrant for the Court performance of Prince Charles's company, Christmas, 1614, was made out to Rowley just as in 1612 and 1613.[44] The warrant for the same date for the Lady Elizabeth's men was made out to Field, showing that the companies were existing as separate units at this time. Prince Charles's men must not have been taken over by Henslowe until he broke the Lady Elizabeth's company again in February, 1615, and sold their stock to 'strangers.' The following Christmas the warrant for the performance by the Prince's men is made out to Alexander Foster, a member of the original company of Lady Elizabeth's men,[45] indicating the amalgamation of the companies. In March, 1616, William Rowley, Thomas Hobbes, and John Newton, formerly of the Prince's company, signed the agreement with Alleyn made by the Henslowe company after Henslowe's death. This agreement sets forth certain terms which are 'accordinge to the former Articles of Agreement had and made with the said Phillip and Jacob,' showing that there had been a previous agreement between Henslowe and the Prince's men.

[42] Greg, *op. cit.,* p. 23.
[43] Murray, *op. cit.* 2. 340.
[44] Cunningham, *op. cit.,* xlii, xliii.
[45] Cunningham, *op. cit.,* p. xl.

Henslowe's company had endured a great deal from March, 1614, to February, 1615, as they show in the *Articles of Grievance* previously referred to. Field, however, had asserted an independent spirit and had fared better than the other members of the company. He received the fifty shillings promised as the allowance for bear-baiting, although the other members were granted only forty shillings; he was also admitted to a share in Henslowe's gallery receipts. But even Field was unable to hold Henslowe to a contract; and in less than a full year after the three-year contract was made, Henslowe broke the company, sold out the stock, took away the hired men, and rendered the company helpless. Certain members of the company remained with Henslowe in spite of his treatment; their names are found in the agreement of the old company with Alleyn, made after Henslowe's death,[46] but Field's name is not in the list. I think that Field's fiery spirit could not be brought to such submission. The usual assumption is that Field went on to the King's company at this time, or between Henslowe's death in January, 1616, and the agreement with Alleyn in the following March. This postulate leaves unexplained the appearance of Field's play, *Amends for Ladies,* performed 'both by the Prince's servants and the Lady Elizabeth's,' at the Blackfriars Theatre. Since this theatre, identified by Fleay with the theatre built in Blackfriars by Rosseter,[47] was hardly completed when the King's order was issued on January 27, 1617, for the destruction of the building,[48] the production of *Amends for Ladies* at the Blackfriars would indicate that Field did not join the King's Men until 1617. Furthermore, we have no evidence of Field's union with that company until 1617, when his name is found in the list of

---

[46] Greg, *op. cit.,* pp. 90-1.

[47] Fleay, *op. cit.,* pp. 263-4.

[48] *Malone Society Collections* I. 374. The order is also quoted by Chambers, *op. cit.* 4. 345, Appendix D, clx.

actors for the *Queen of Corinth.* I think that Field and such members of the Henslowe company as are not accounted for by the agreement with Alleyn (with the exception of Robert Pallant, who rejoined Queen Anne's men in the provinces by May 6, 1615) rejoined Rosseter and travelled in the provinces under the old patent for the Children of the Queen's Revels, for after a period of two years this company is again found as a separate unit, playing in the provinces.[49]

On June 3, 1615, Rosseter secured a License for the erection of a theatre in Blackfriars for 'the Children of the Revels for the tyme being of the Queenes Maiestie and for the Prince's Players and for the ladie Elizabeth's Players.'[50] Light is thrown on the inclusion of the Prince's servants and the Lady Elizabeth's with the Revels company, by the answer of Edmund Traves and Susanna, his wife, to the bill of complaint of Edward Alleyn, dated June 30, 1623.[51] From this document it appears that in spite of Rosseter's withdrawal from Henslowe's company, 1614, Henslowe had become connected with the enterprise in his usual capacity as financier. The company probably anticipated being in the new theatre for the winter, but complaint was made against the erection of another theatre in Blackfriars, especially since it would 'adjoyne so neare unto the Church in Blackfriars as it would disturb and interrupt the Congregation at divine seruice upon the week dayes.'[52] On September 26, 1615, the work was stopped by an order from the Lord Mayor, and the statement was made that any further work done toward converting the building into a playhouse would be punished by imprisonment. That active measures for suppressing this theatre were taken is shown by an entry in the *Repertories of the Court of Common*

[49] Murray, *op. cit.* 2. 246.
[50] *Malone Society Collections* I. 277-8.
[51] Hillebrand, *The Child Actors,* p. 246.
[52] *Malone Society Collections* I. 373-4.

Council, September 28, 1615,[53] for the Chamberlain was ordered to reimburse the City's Remembrancer the sum of £30, 16s., and 6d., spent by him in 'the restraint of building of the playhouse at puddle wharfe.' This unexpected trouble meant that another period of travel must be undergone by the company. In February, 1616, a reward was given to the 'players of ye Queen's Revells' in Nottingham;[54] in June the company was back at Coventry.[55]

During this year, work was again begun on Rosseter's theatre. Miss Gildersleeve suggests that since Lord Chief Justice Coke stopped the work on a mere legal quibble, there was no reason why Rosseter could not carry out his original plan after Coke's removal in 1616.[56] Rosseter's license had granted that he should be allowed to 'play exercise and practise' the members of the three companies in Porter's Hall, 'Any lawe Statute Act of Parliament restraint or any other matter or thing whatsoever to the contrary notwithstanding,'[57] and so it may be that he contended the injunction of the Lord Mayor and was able to proceed with the work under the direct authority of the King. When the theatre was sufficiently completed for the production of plays, Field and his associates had a great reunion under the kindly care of Rosseter and produced Field's *Amends for Ladies,* which had belonged to the Whitefriars company of the Children. But the theatre was ill-fated. Since Rosseter had continued building 'notwithstanding diverse Commaundments and prohibicons to the contrary,' on January 27, 1617, the King himself, through the Council, 'signifyed his pleasure that the same shalbee pulled downe; so as it bee made vnfitt for any such vse.'[58] In February the Children of the Queen's

---

[53] Hillebrand, *op. cit.* 2. 502.
[54] Murray, *op. cit.* 2. 376.
[55] *Ibid.* 2. 246.
[56] V. C. Gildersleeve, *Government Regulation of the Elizabethan Drama* (New York, 1908), pp. 199-200.
[57] *Malone Society Collections* 1. 278.
[58] *Ibid.* 1. 374.

Revels reappeared in the provinces, but Field was no longer with them. After four very unsettled years, he is found with the King's Men. On March 20, 1617, the Lady Elizabeth's company was granted a new license, stating that henceforth there was to be only one company by that name. The Prince's men appeared intermittently until 1623, when they are found at the Curtain Theatre to which they may have gone in 1617.

During his short period of connection with the King's Men, Field became a shareholder in the Globe Theatre. The *Ostler-Hemings* lawsuit (1615-6)[59] sets a downward limit for the date, as Field was not then a sharer; the *Witter-Hemings* document of April 28, 1619, however, names Field as a shareholder.[60]

After the Livery Allowance of May, 1619,[61] Field's name is not found among the King's Men. He did not act in *Barnavelt*, August, 1619. Probably he was dead, though letters of administration were not granted to his sister until August, 1620. The vacancy caused by Field's death was filled by John Rice, who, however, had only minor rôles. It is possible that John Rice was a relative, or even son, of Field's sister, Dorcas, who married Edward Rice in 1590.

Beginning at the age of thirteen, Field was an actor for nineteen years, during which time he was associated with four leading dramatic companies. In spite of his Puritan descent he possessed great theatrical talent, and achieved immediate success among the Children at Blackfriars. Even in the earliest play in which he is known to have acted, *Cynthia's Revels* (1600), he took the leading rôle, for his name heads the list of the six 'principall Comoedians' of the play. He held the place of foremost actor with the company of the Children of the Revels both at Blackfriars and at

[59] Wallace, 'Shakespeare in London,' *The Times,* October 2 and 4, 1909.

[60] Wallace, *Shakespeare and His London Associates,* p. 63.

[61] *Report of the Historical Manuscripts Commission* 4. 299.

Whitefriars. His name is given first in the list of actors of Jonson's *Poetaster* (1601) and *Epicoene* (1609-10). We feel safe in assuming that he had the leading rôle in *Bartholomew Fair* (1614). In this play Jonson compliments Field, placing him in comparison with Burbadge: when Cokes is looking at the puppets, which Littlewit calls a Children's company, he asks:

> Which is your Burbadge now? . . . Your best actor, your Field? (Act V. 3).

Field's name is also given first in the list of actors for Beaumont and Fletcher's *Coxcomb* (1611) and *Honest Man's Fortune* (1613). In the prologue of the 1641 edition of Chapman's *Bussy D'Ambois* there is a tribute to Field's fame as actor in the title rôle of this play: the speaker says, 'Field is gone whose action first did give it name.' Even after Field joined the King's Men and tested his powers by competition with more experienced actors, he ranked second only to Burbadge. His name appears next to Burbadge's in the actor-lists of the *Queen of Corinth* and the *Loyal Subject,* and though it falls to third place in the *Knight of Malta* and to fifth in the *Mad Lover,* this order is probably occasioned by the suitability of the rôles for Field. His name appears in the list of original actors of Shakespeare's plays, given in the first folio, but we do not know in what rôles he played. Malone says that he 'probably at the Globe and Blackfriars Theatres performed female parts.'[62] He adds, however, that when 'he became too manly to represent the characters of women, he played the part of Bussy D'Ambois in Chapman's play of that name.' These two statements seem inconsistent. Field's portrait shows that he was of slight build and feminine appearance, and it may

---

[62] Malone, *Variorum* 3. 213. T. W. Baldwin argues that Field took youthful male rôles, playing opposite Burbadge—Miranda to Mountferrat, etc. (*The Shakespearean Company.* Princeton University Press, 1927, pp. 204-7.)

be that he was able to 'speak small' and continue in female rôles, as did Kynaston later. It is at least interesting to think of him as playing leading lady to Burbadge's heroes.

Field's reputation lasted far beyond his own day. Henry Vaughan associates Field's acting with that of Swanston, who also possessed great histrionic ability and took prominent rôles in the Beaumont-Fletcher plays. In his poem *Upon Mr. Fletcher's Plays,* he writes:[63]

> Thou dost but kill, and circumvent in jest;
> And when thy anger'd Muse swells to a blow
> 'Tis but for Field's or Swansteed's overthrow.

In 1664 Richard Flecknoe says, 'In this time were poets and actors in their greatest flourish: Jonson and Shakespeare, with Beaumont and Fletcher, their poets and Field and Burbage, their actors.'[64] Apparently, then, Field measured up to Heywood's standard for a good actor. Heywood thought 'actors should be men pick'd out personable, according to the parts they present: they should be rather schollers, that, though they cannot speake well, know how to speake, or else to have that volubility that they can speake well, though they understand not what, and so both imperfections may by instructions be helped and amended: but where a good tongue and a good conceit both faile, there can never be a good actor.'[65] Field was a scholar, possessed of both 'a good tongue and a good conceit,' and he used one to the benefit of the other, so that he was able to take his place among the actors of the first rank.

[63] H. Vaughan, *Works*, ed. Martin 1. 55.

[64] R. Flecknoe, *Short Discourse of the English Stage*, in *The English Drama and Stage under the Tudor and Stuart Princes, 1543-1664* (Printed for the Roxburghe Library, London, 1869), p. 277.

[65] T. Heywood, *An Apology for Actors* (1612). Printed for the Shakespeare Society (London, 1841), p. 43.

CHAPTER III

FIELD'S LATER PRIVATE LIFE

We know very little of Field's private life during the nineteen years of his connection with dramatic companies. There are three interesting letters from Field to Henslowe, which seem to belong to the year 1613, and throw light on Field's relationship with Henslowe and on his financial condition at the time.[1] One of the letters is a request for £10 for a play being written by Daborne and Field. It is a good example of Field's diplomatic handling of Henslowe. He speaks confidently about the success of the play, says Daborne may have his request of another company, and holds out the hope that a little more assistance will put them in position to pay all that they owe: 'You know the last money you disburst was justly pay'd in,' he says, 'and we are now in a way to pay you all so, unlesse your selfe, for want of a small supplie, will put us out of it againe.' In a second letter Field says that he has been 'unluckily taken on an execution of £30.' He asks Henslowe for £10, and promises, 'I will never share penny till you have it againe.' He again assumes the half-complimentary, half-threatening tone: 'I am loath to importune, because I know your disbursements are great; nor must any know I send to you, for then my creditor will not free me but for the whole some. I pray, speedily consider my occasion, for if I be putt to use other means, I hope all men and yourself will excuse me if (inforcedly) I cannot proove so honest, as towards you I ever resolved to be.' The third letter is signed by Field, Daborne, and Massinger but is written by Field. The three playwrights are asking for £5 without which they cannot be bailed. Field says, 'I do not think you so void of Chris-

[1] Greg, *Henslowe Papers,* pp. 65-7, 84.

tianitie, but that you would throw so much money into the Thames as wee request now of you; rather than endanger so many innocent lives.' He calls Henslowe's attention to the fact that if he is not bailed, he cannot play, and says, 'It will loose you £20 ere the end of the nexte weeke, besides the hinderance of the next new play.' He closes with the petition, 'Pray consider our cases with humanitie, and now give us cause to acknowledge you our true friend in time of need.'

Field evidently stood high in the good grace of Henslowe. He signs his letters 'loving son,' and addresses one of them to 'Father Hinchlow.' He seems to have known just how to handle the eccentric manager. The quotations above show that he always devotes a part of the letter to being conciliatory: he praises Henslowe's humanity, apologizes for troubling him, or recalls the true friendship that Henslowe has shown in the past. He shows that the loan will be profitable in the end and is only a temporary and comparatively small output for certain definite returns. Evidently such a method was very successful, for the most urgent request, the one signed by the three playwrights, received an immediate response; the messenger, Robert Davison, carried the money back to the imprisoned men. Field's financial status at this time presents a contrast to his somewhat boastful declaration that he will not dedicate his *Woman is a Weathercock* to anyone because 'forty shillings I care not for.' Although in 1613 he had written both his plays, the price of a play, which seems to have varied from ten to twenty pounds, was not sufficient to make him independent of Henslowe.

Field formed some very interesting friendships during his career as actor and playwright. He acted in the plays of Jonson, Chapman, Marston, Beaumont, and Fletcher when these playwrights were the dramatists of his company, and, naturally enough, established friendly relations with all of them. He was closely associated with Daborne,

Fletcher, and Massinger in the collaborative writing of plays. Agreements were made in an hour of social cheer, for the feeling was current that 'drink must clap up the bargain.' The reading of new plays before Alleyn and others afforded another occasion for a cup of canary, and many entries in Henslowe's diary show that he furnished the money for 'good cheer' at the Mermaid. The celebration of a first performance was probably the time when the wine flowed most freely and spirits ran high. As a protégé of Jonson and a prominent actor, Field was, no doubt, a well-known figure at these gatherings of the dramatists. From his plays we see that he had the ability to make a quick and often pert retort that would make him a pleasing addition to the brilliant company which often assembled in the taverns near the theatres.

In 1616 Field was suffering personally from the Puritan attacks on the stage. Mr. Sutton, the preacher at St. Mary Overy, Southwark, had not only denounced plays and players but had openly attacked Field. In his *Remonstrance*,[2] Nathan says: 'You have bene of late pleased, and that many tymes from the Holy Hill of Sion, the pulpitt, a place sanctified and dedicated for the winning not discouraging of souls, to send forth many those bitter breathinges, those uncharitable and unlimited curses of condemnacions, against that poore calling it hath pleased the Lord to place me in, that my spiritt is moved; the fire is kindled and I must speak; and the rather because you have not spared in the extraordinary violence of your passion, particularly to point att me and some other of my quallity, and directly to our faces in the publique assembly to pronounce us dampned, as thoughe you meant to send us alive to hell in the sight of many witnesses.' Field defended himself with a great deal of logic and piety, and absolutely refused to be damned, pointing out that in the Bible he had found only

[2] Halliwell-Phillipps, *Illustrations*, pp. 115-6.

'conjurors, sorcerers, and witches, *ipso facto,* damned.' He especially resented this attack because he and a number of his friends—Fletcher, Massinger, Henslowe, Ecclestone, Taylor, John Rice, and others—were parishioners of St. Mary's.[3] He reminded Sutton that he had no hesitancy in accepting their contributions, no matter how much he seemed to 'despise the man that gaynes it or the wayes he gettes it.' Field assured Sutton of his belief that Christ died for 'all men's sinnes not excepting the player,' and accused Sutton of hindering him from the sacrament and attempting to banish him from his 'owne parishe Church.' It may have been at this time that he withdrew from St. Mary's; at the time of his death, about three years later, he was a parishioner of St. Giles-in-the-Fields.[4]

A few anecdotes in regard to Field's life while he was a player have come down to us. Though it is unlikely that they are authentic, they make interesting reading. John Taylor, in his *Wit and Mirth,*[5] gives one which is merely a play on the word *post,* and has been attached to more than one name:

> Master Field the Player, riding vp Fleet street a great pace, a Gentleman called him, and asked him, what play was played that day. Hee (being angry to be stayed vpon so friuoulous a demand) answered, that he might see what Play was to be played vpon euery Poste. I cry you mercy (said the Gentleman), I tooke you for a Poste, you road so faste.

In Pierce's *Field Genealogy* there is a little skit on the spelling of Field's name.[6] Though the nineteenth century flavor of the jest is quite evident, we may enjoy it and admit that

[3] W. Rendle, 'Sacramental Token Books at St. Savior's, Southwark,' in *The Genealogist,* New Series 1. 15-21 (1884). Cf. W. Thompson, *Southwark Cathedral* (London, 1906), p. 270.
[4] *Admon. Act Book,* P. C. C., 2 August, 1620.
[5] J. Taylor, *Wit and Mirth,* in Hazlitt's *Shakespeare Jest-Books* (London, 1864) 3. 24-5.
[6] F. C. Pierce, *Field Genealogy* (Chicago, 1901), pp. 24-5.

if Field had lived two centuries later, his wit might have taken this form:

> A nobleman connected with him, but whose branch of the family spelled their name Feild, asked him how this difference in spelling the name came about. 'I do not know,' said Nat, 'unless it was because my branch of the family was the first that learned to spell.

Collier quotes a punning epigram, which was current in commonplace books of the day.[7] It is entitled *Nathaniell Feild suspected for too much familiarity with his M^rs. Lady May.* The spelling of the name indicates either that the actor is not the subject of this epigram or that the confusion in regard to names had already arisen.

A letter found among the papers of James Hay, Earl of Carlisle, when he was ambassador to Germany, indicates that in 1619 Field was having first-hand experience with the weathercock-type of woman. William Trumbull, Ambassador to Holland, wrote to Hay from Brussels on June 5, telling all the latest gossip that he had heard from England. He reports that the Earl of Argyll 'was privy to the payment of 15 or 16 poundes sterling to one of your lordships Trayne called Wisedome for the noursing of a childe which the world sayes is daughter to my lady (Argyll) and N(at) Feild the Player.'[8] Lady Argyll's sister, the wife of Sir Richard Farmer, had been in trouble in 1617 because 'one Onlay, a young dancing reveller, of the Temple' had been visiting her too frequently;[9] so it would seem that the family was not above infidelity.

An epigram, giving Field as the actor of the rôle of

---

[7] Collier, *English Dramatic Poetry and Annals of the Stage* 3. 434-5.

[8] E. J. L. Scott, *Athenæum* 1. 103 (1882).

[9] T. Birch, *The Court and Times of James the First* (London, 1848) 2. 7.

Othello, is quoted by Collier from a manuscript which, he
says, was among those of Mr. Heber:[10]

> Field is, in sooth, an actor—all men *know it,*
> And is the true Othello of the *poet.*
> I wonder if 'tis true, as people tell us,
> That, like the character, he is jealous.
> If it be so, and many living swear it,
> It takes no little from the actor's merit,
> Since, as the Moor is jealous of his wife,
> Field can display the passion to the life.

One cannot feel that the epigram was a contemporary production; both metre and expression have a strangely non-
Elizabethan sound. Doubt is cast upon the authenticity by
the fact that the general tone is the same as that in some
additional lines on Burbadge's rôle of Othello, which Collier gives from a manuscript, for *An Elegy on Our Late
Protean Roscius Richard Burbage.*[11] Othello was one of
Burbadge's great rôles; and since both Burbadge and Field
were playing with the King's Men, certainly Field would not
take this rôle during Burbadge's lifetime. He was with
the company only a short time after Burbadge's death,
scarcely long enough to become known as 'the true
Othello of the poet.' Field may have played Desdemona to
Burbadge's Othello, but only Collier could imagine his playing Othello! The fundamental error, however, is the error
in the point on which the entire commendation is based.
Since the actor was a *bachelor,* Collier's fabrication misses
the point.

Though I have been unable to ascertain the exact date
of Field's death, this date is now fixed between May 19,
1619, when his name appears in the *Livery Allowance* for
the King's Men, and August 2, 1620, when *Letters of
Administration* for the goods of Nathan Field were granted

[10] Collier, *op. cit.* 3. 437.
[11] Collier, *New Particulars Regarding the Works of Shakespeare*
(London, 1836), pp. 29-31.

to Dorcas, the first child of John Field, and wife of Edward Rice.[12] Since he did not play in *Barnavelt*, August, 1619, I surmise that he had withdrawn from the theatre and may already have died.[13]

With this brief notice our knowledge of Field ends. His picture, which hangs in the Master's official residence at Dulwich College, is quaintly listed as, 'Master Feild's picture in his shirt; on a board, in a black frame, fileted with gold; an actor.'[14]

[12] *Admon. Act Book,* P. C. C. 2 August, 1620. See Appendix.

[13] C. L. Lockert, 'A Scene in *The Fatal Dowry,' Mod. Lang. Notes,* May, 1920, shows that Field did not complete the regular alternation with Massinger in the collaborative writing of this play and connects this fact with Field's retirement from the stage. Probably Field's death accounts for both his incomplete work on the play and his disappearance from the theatre.

[14] G. F. Warner, *Catalogue of the Manuscripts and Muniments of Dulwich College* (London, 1881), p. 207.

CHAPTER IV

FIELD'S INDIVIDUAL WORK AS DRAMATIST

It required the indomitable egotism of youth to lead Field to conceive of writing plays in competition with the imposing array of 'fellows and followers of Shakespeare.' When Field began writing, probably in 1609, Shakespeare himself was still writing, Dekker and Heywood were at the height of fame, Middleton was producing, and Beaumont and Fletcher had entered the dramatic lists. Through nine years of acting, Field was thoroughly familiar with the plays of the leading poets of his own company, Marston, Chapman, and Jonson. By 1609 Marston's work was complete; Chapman had written his comedies, as well as *Bussy D'Ambois* and the two *Biron* plays; Jonson had already produced eight of his plays and was writing the *Alchemist*.

Field was only twenty-two when he decided to become a playwright. The first indication that he was interested in writing drama is found in his commendatory verses prefixed to Fletcher's *Faithfull Shepherdess*, published between January and July, 1609.[1] In these verses he speaks of having talked with Fletcher privately about writing, and now publicly confesses:

> . . . . . . my ambition is
> To live to perfect such a work as this.

Fletcher and Beaumont, who was only two or three years older than Field, had just begun to write plays, and it may be that it was their success that stirred Field's ambition. In 1609 the Children's company was experiencing a lull in activity, for the Blackfriars Theatre had been taken over by the King's Men, and the Children of the Revels had no

[1] C. M. Gayley, *Beaumont, the Dramatist* (New York, 1914), p. 304.

permanent home. Robert Keysar was holding the company
together, however, with the expectation of their playing
again after the cessation of the plague. Evans had dismissed many of the poets of the company, and new plays
would be needed when the company renewed its activity.
Field had a good eye for business, and it seems very likely
that he looked upon the situation as offering an opportune
opening for him. His first play, *Woman is a Weathercock,*
purports to be undertaken in the spirit of retaliation. In
his prefatory letter to the reader, Field says: 'I have been
vexed with vile plays myself a great while, hearing many;
now I thought to be even with some, and they should hear
mine too.' He put together a clever assortment of situations, phrases, and words, taken over from the plays in
which he had played, combined with these some of the popular sentiments and characters of the day, added his personal
animus toward women, and threw over all of this his own
exuberant personality. He did not overestimate his ability
when he decided to write, for his play was one of the successful productions acted by the Children of the Revels after
they were established in Whitefriars. Field did so well, in
fact, that his ability was recognized by his contemporaries,
and he was received by them as a valuable assistant in collaborative work. Since he was greater as a practical playwright than as a creative genius, he gave up individual
composition after writing two plays and was satisfied to
collaborate with Beaumont, Fletcher, and Massinger, placing
his technical skill at the service of those with greater genius
than he possessed.

Although *Woman is a Weathercock* was not printed until
1612, it was entered in the *Stationers' Register* on November
23, 1611. All evidence points to its being written 1609-10,
and acted in 1610. In the address to the reader, Field says,
'I send you a comedy here as good as I could *then* make.'
This in itself leads us to infer that the play had been written
some time before it was presented for publication. An up-

ward limit for the date of the play is given by Field's own
statement in his complimentary poem to Fletcher, mentioned
previously. Here he speaks of himself as one:

> Whose unknown name and muse in swathing clowtes,
> Is not yet grown to strenth, among these rankes
> To have a roome.

In the second scene of Act I there are three allusions to
the Cleve wars (1609 ff.), and in the first scene of Act II, a
reference to the plague, which indicate that Field had begun
writing in 1609. The title page states that the play was
'acted before the King in Whitehall. And divers times
privately at the Whitefriars by the Children of her Majesties
Revels.' The only opportunity for the production before
the King in Whitehall was during the Christmas season of
1609-10, for the Children of the Revels did not appear at
Court in the winter of 1610-11. Though the Children were
probably established in the Whitefriars some time in 1609,
the patent allowing them to resume the title of the 'Children
of the Queen's Revels,' the name of which they had been
deprived in 1605, was not granted until January 4, 1610.
It seems, therefore, that the play must have been acted the
'divers times' at Whitefriars during 1610 and 1611.

At the time that *Woman is a Weathercock* was published,
it seems that Field was writing *Amends for Ladies* as an
antidote for his first dramatic effort, although it was not
published until 1618. In the dedication of his first play
Field addressed any woman that had been constant and
begged her to 'continue so but till my next play be *printed,*
wherein she shall see what amends I *have made* to her and
all the sex.' It will be noticed that he speaks of printing
rather than of writing the play and mentions the amends
as having already been made. This early date is supported
by a reference which points to the title of Field's play, found
in Stafford's *Niobe Dissolv'd into a Nilus,* entered in the
Stationers' Register on October 10, 1611. The words, 'I
will never write an Amends for Woman till I see women

amended,' indicate that Stafford thought Field had made a great mistake in choice of subject for his new play! There is one difficulty that must be explained in regard to accepting the early date. The source of that part of the plot which treats of the testing of the wife's fidelity by the jealous husband is the *Curious Impertinent* story from Don Quixote.[2] The first English translation of *Don Quixote* was entered in the *Stationers' Register* January 19, 1611, but it was not printed until 1612. Since we have no right to assume that Field could read Spanish, it becomes necessary to explain his knowledge of the story anterior to the English edition. Thomas Shelton states that he had made his translation five or six years before the publication. Ben Jonson refers to *Don Quixote* in *Epicoene* when Dauphine is said to be living on *Amadis de Gaul* and *Don Quixote;*[3] so it is possible that Jonson knew the Shelton translation in manuscript, and that Field had access to it through him. In 1608 there appeared in Paris a French translation of the *Curious Impertinent* story, made by N. Baudouin. From one source or the other the story was known to a number of dramatists prior to 1612.[4] The *Second Maiden's Tragedy,* licensed with reformations on October 31, 1611, is a close parallel to the Cervantes story. Chapman in the *Widow's Tears* made use of the idea of the testing of the wife by the jealous husband. Beaumont and Fletcher's *Coxcomb* bears some resemblance to the *Curious Impertinent* story. Field had acted in both the latter plays. When Love-all reveals to Subtle his plan for testing the Lady Bright, Subtle addresses Love-all as 'dear Coxcomb,' indicating, possibly, that Field had the Beaumont-Fletcher play

[2] H. Fischer, *Nathaniel Field's Komödie 'Amends for Ladies'* (Kiel, 1907), pp. 32-3.

[3] Act IV. 1.

[4] A. S. N. Rosenbach, 'The *Curious Impertinent* in English Dramatic Literature before Shelton's Translation of *Don Quixote'*, *Mod. Lang. Notes* 17. 357-67 (1902).

in mind. Since Field could readily have heard the Cervantes story if he had found no opportunity to read it,
and since he had acted in a version of the story in *Widow's
Tears,* the late date of printing of Shelton's translation does
not mean that *Amends* was not written until after 1612.
The appearance of Moll Cutpurse in Act II. 1 may be due
to the influence of Middleton and Dekker's *Roaring Girl,*
another indication that the date of the play should be placed
about 1611. The title page mentions only the performances
at the Blackfriars, where it was given 'both by the Prince's
servants and the Lady Elizabeth's.' As we have already
seen, this means the production at Rosseter's Blackfriars
during the year previous to the publication of the play, and
so does not help us with the problem of its date of composition. I think, however, that we may conclude that *Amends
for Ladies* followed *Woman is a Weathercock* very closely
and was first presented by the Children of the Queen's
Revels at Whitefriars.

Woman is a Weathercock appears in only one quarto
(that of 1612): there are two early editions of *Amends for
Ladies,* the first in 1618 and the second in 1639. In the
second edition the title page bears the additional words, 'with
the merry prankes of Moll Cutpurse, or the humour of roaring: a Comedy full of honest wit and mirth.' There is no
revision of the text, however, and the change in the title
is evidently only an effort to arouse interest. Fortunately
both plays are very accessible, since they appear in four
collections of old plays as well as in separate editions by
Collier.[5]

One of the most noticeable characteristics of Field as
playwright is his great skill in plotting. He successfully

[5] a. Collier's *Five Old Plays* (1833).
b. *Nero and Other Plays,* Mermaid Series (1888).
c. *Old English Drama,* vol. 2 (1830).
d. Dodsley's *Old Plays,* vol. 13 (3rd ed.).
e. Edited separately by Collier (1829).

conducts a highly involved intrigue to perfect untanglement, and does not lose a single thread of the plot by the wayside. *Woman is a Weathercock* is a single intrigue, built up of three tricks which, though known to the audience, complicate life for the characters. Sir John Worldly arranges financially successful marriages for two of his daughters, Bellafront and Kate. By counterfeiting the parson, Neville saves Bellafront for her true lover, Scudmore, and Kate for himself. Sir Abraham Ninny, the suitor of Lucida, Sir John's third daughter, is gulled into marrying a loose waiting-woman, Mistress Wagtail, and so Lucida is left free to console Count Frederick when he is forsaken by Bellafront. Captain Pouts is tricked into a recantation of his slander of Kate by Kate's pseudo-husband and is sent back to the wars with a sword for his mistress. The use of disguise adds to the complexity of the story. A single character sometimes assumes more than one disguise: Neville appears twice as a parson and once as a vizard maker; Scudmore assumes the rôle of a servant in the first act and of Neville in the last act. Disguise plays an important part in the manipulation of the plot. By disguise Neville prevents the validity of Bellafront's marriage to Count Frederick, and Strange forces Captain Pouts to confess that he has slandered Kate. It is also by disguise that Scudmore gains access to Bellafront and, finally, in the concluding masque succeeds in eloping with her. Through all the entanglements which Field brings about, he very skilfully keeps the audience informed as to what is going on and which characters are in disguise. His work shows that he had the story planned in advance, so that the solution could easily be contrived in the masque scene.

Amends for Ladies is even more intricate in structure than *Weathercock*. There is a treble plot to which are added several episodes and a number of tricks. The three stories of almost equal interest are: Subtle's testing of the fidelity of Sir John Love-all's wife, based on the *Curious*

Impertinent narrative; Bold's attempts to win the widow; and Ingen's efforts to gain the maid. The episodes appear to be wholly gratuitous. They have no direct connection with the plots and were probably added for their popular appeal. The appearance of Moll Cut-Purse, the portrayal of Lord Feesimple's initiation into the mysteries of 'roaring,' and the duping of the old Count into consenting to marry his own son, disguised as a woman, all make good stage business. The outcome of the Lady Bright-Bold and the Lady Honour-Ingen stories is dependent upon tricks and disguise. In his effort to win Lady Bright, Bold takes the rôle of waiting maid, but is discovered and repulsed. Converted by Lady Bright's honor, and in despair of securing her consent to marry him, he tricks Lord Feesimple into thinking that the widow has consented to marriage with Feesimple, if he will appear at the church disguised as a woman. Once there, Bold pretends to Lady Bright that he is to marry this woman, in reality Lord Feesimple, and makes her give her consent to his marrying the woman of his choice. He then claims the no longer resisting Lady Bright as his choice! Ingen, in order to win the hard-hearted Lady Honour, resorts to a pretended marriage with his brother in disguise. Lady Honour then complicates matters by assuming the rôle of an Irish footboy in Ingen's household, but finally has to reveal herself in order to stop a duel between her brother and Ingen, who is accused of being responsible for Lady Honour's disappearance. Lord Proudly then defeats Ingen's hopes by reporting that he has arranged a marriage between his sister and Lord Feesimple's father. He is outwitted, however, just before the ceremony, for Lady Honour feigns illness and is married to the physician summoned, who proves to be no other than Ingen in disguise.

The situations which Field employs in his plays are the stock situations of the period: confusion arising from disguise, tavern brawls, duels, attempts on virtue, last scene conversions, and marriages that do not hold because they are performed by someone who is only disguised as a parson, or because the bride's femininity is restricted to dress alone. Field's original contribution is the skilful manipulation of old material, and the vivacity with which it is handled.

Field uses expectation rather than surprise as a dramatic motive, except that he reserves the right to give us one surprise in the fifth act. In *Woman is a Weathercock* we have not been prepared for Kate's rejection of Strange and sudden choice of Neville; in *Amends for Ladies* the gulling of old Count Feesimple comes as a surprise. All usage of tricks and disguise is carefully explained to the audience, so that there is no difficulty in following what is taking place. The exposition in the first scene is full and clear; and as further explanation becomes necessary, it is given either in expository soliloquies or by means of asides and parenthetical statements. Field was a painstaking craftsman and carried his audience ahead of the action on the stage by means of forward-looking hints and inconspicuous bits of preparation. These are not given so far ahead that their significance is lost, as is so often the case with Brome, but appear as a forewarning of something that follows almost immediately. For example, in Act IV. 3 of *Amends* Lady Honour pretends to consent to Lord Proudly's arrangement for her marriage with Count Feesimple, but she whispers with Ingen when she tells him good-bye and explains in an aside that she has to acquiesce to prevent the continuation of the duel. The audience is then on tiptoe with the anticipation of some means by which Lady Honour can escape her brother's decree. A part of the pleasure of the audience at the untanglement comes because each one present is made to feel a thrill of satisfaction at his own cleverness in being able to see through the disguise of physician and parson and to recognize Lady Honour's illness as her whispered scheme. In *Weathercock*, Act IV. 1, Neville explains to Scudmore that his chance to gain Bellafront will come

during the masque if he will learn Neville's part, wear the
costume in which Neville is expected to appear, and follow
'further directions.' In Act V. 1, the 'further directions'
are given in a very skilful bit of dialogue between Neville
and Scudmore. When the masque begins, the audience is
eagerly watching to see Scudmore and Bellafront steal away,
although the characters in the play do not notice their disappearance for some time.

Coming at the time that he did, Field is naturally a dramatist of humours and manners. He portrays the jealous
husband, the half-dead old nobleman who will take any
gentlewoman with delight, the hypocritical Puritan, the
counterfeit soldier, the parasite, the worldly man, the melancholy character, the bawd, the inconstant woman, the foolish
young man who would become a roarer, the newly-created
knight, and a whole family of Ninnies, one of whom
poetizes for good measure. This is quite an array of the
stock characters of London society. Field's most original
character is the sprightly page, who delights the audience
with his pert asides. The character portrayal is external
and reveals the author's visualization of the characters
rather than his omniscience as to their inner being. The
characters do not act from complex motives or analyze their
own actions; they appear to be manipulated by the playwright so that they will carry on the story that he has in
mind. In spite of these facts, however, his characters do
possess a fair degree of personality; they are not merely
humours. His women are abstractions, representing inconstancy in *Weathercock* and constancy in *Amends,* yet they
are distinguishable one from another. Lady Honour has an
especial personal charm, and, as a page recounting the virtues
and the grief of her lady, has something of the appeal which
Julia and Viola possess.

As a writer of comedy of manners, Field is in close touch
with contemporary life. He creates an illusion of actuality
by local references, by realistic pictures of contemporary life

and customs, and by references to events and to literature
of his day.   The scenes of each play are in or near London,
and the locality is made perfectly definite by the use of the
names of real streets and places.   In *Weathercock* there are
references to eleven places in and around London, and in
Amends to eight, some of which are mentioned more than
once.   These are: Pickedhatch, Pancras, the ducking ponds
at Islington, Lambeth Fields, Moorfields, Bear Tavern,
Paul's, Newgate, Bridewell, Cheapside, the Fortune, Newington Butts, Turnbull Street, Fleet Street, Pie Corner in
Smithfield, Blackfriars, and Gravesend.   Certain scenes
help to make us acquainted with the manners of the seventeenth century.   The tavern scene in which Lord Feesimple
becomes a roarer was probably drawn from a real model;
and it is to be feared that Whorebang, Bots, Tearchaps, and
Spillblood were contemporary characters.   Sir John Melton
has described such characters as frequenting taverns: 'The
Fierie Devill, is your Roaring Boy, that like a Salamander
lives most commonly by Fire; Smoake is the chiefest
nourishment hee hath: hee is a swearing Rascall, that with
the hot Oathes he spues out from the Canon of his mouth,
is able to burne, if not his owne, yet their lippes that stand
by them.   This Spirit is most commonly resident in Tobacco
Shops, Hot-Water Shops, Taverns, Brothels, and such
Places.'[6]   Lord Feesimple's suggestion that they go out
and break windows shows that the popularity of this sport
had not waned since the day of Surrey.   The scene in Seldom's shop might easily have been duplicated any day, for
many shop-keepers had their wives stay in the shop to attract
trade.   Not many of the keepers, however, had such
virtuous wives as Grace Seldom.   Certain customs in connection with marriages are given by Field.   After his pretended marriage Ingen follows the seventeenth century custom of sending gloves to all his friends who were absent

---

[6] Melton, Sir John, *The Astrologaster* (London, 1620), p. 72.

from the ceremony. The wedding dinner and the wedding masque presented in *Weathercock* portray the usual festivities accompanying marriage. The gallants of the time affected either extreme nicety in dress or an equally studied carelessness. Field satirizes this concern about dress in some of his most effective scenes. The tailor-and-lord scene in *Weathercock* (Act I. 2), showing the time and pains taken by the tailor in dressing Count Frederick for his wedding and the admiring comments of the Count's followers, is excellent comedy. Master Pert in *Amends* (Act III. 3) does not enjoy the play that he is attending because 'one of the purls of his band was fallen out of his reach to order again.' One of the disasters of the duel between Ingen and Lord Proudly is that Lord Proudly's cutwork band is endangered. Bold, on the other hand, 'spends as much time to make himself slovenly, as the other to be spruce' (*Amends*, Act III. 3). The prevalence of 'dainty oaths' in these plays is sufficient to give one an extensive Jacobean swearing vocabulary. Stubbes was horrified at the innumerable oaths of the day, for, he says: 'Wee take in vaine abuse, and blaspheme, the sacred name of God in our ordenarie talke, for euery light trifle . . . . By continuall vse whereof, it is growne to this perfection, that at euery other worde, you shal heare either woundes, bloud, sides, harte, nailes, foot, or some other part of Christes blessed bodie, yea, sometymes no parte thereof shalbe left vntorne of these bloudie Villaines. And to sweare by God at euery worde.'[7] Field uses them all, and, like Anaides in *Cynthia's Revels,* he might have said, 'I have more oaths than I know how to utter, by this air.' There are also some references which are interesting in connection with the theatre. The poor conceits associated with the theatre at Newington Butts are alluded to by Pendant (*Weathercock,* Act III. 3). The Fortune Theatre is mentioned twice: Lord Feesimple desires to go to the

---

[7] P. Stubbes, *Anatomy of Abuses* (London, 1877-9), pp. 132-3.

Fortune to see *Long Meg* and the *Ship* (*Amends*, Act II. 1) ;
the Drawer at the tavern reports that all the gentlewomen
in that section 'went to see a play at the Fortune, and are
not come in yet,' and that it is thought 'they sup with the
players' (*Amends*, Act III. 4). The manner in which
players delivered their lines is referred to when Lord
Proudly compliments Frank on the delivery of his speech
and asks if he had ever been a player (*Amends*, Act V. 2).
The subjects chosen for plays are spoken of several times.
Scudmore mentions the plays in which is found 'a maid's
inconstancy presented to the life' (*Weathercock*, Act.
III. 2) ; Lady Perfect questions the justice of presenting
women only as the 'degraded subject of these plays'
(*Amends*, Act II. 3). Strange feels that his deed has been
notable enough for him to hope to live 'to see the day, it
shall be shown to people in a play' (*Weathercock*, Act V. 2) ;
but Kate does not feel that it is a compliment for a citizen
to be represented in a play, and threatens Strange with
thinking of him as :

> ....such a citizen
> As the plays flout still, and is made the subject
> Of all the stages.
>   *Weathercock*, Act II. 1.

The way in which playmakers got copy is given when
Whorebang warns Welltried that the Roarers will have no
'observers.' Welltried assures him, however, that he is no
playmaker (*Amends*, Act III. 4). In *Amends* (Act II. 4)
there is an interesting allusion to the necessity of a woman's
having an escort when she attended a play. Welltried suggests that perhaps Lady Honour has stolen out to see a
play, but Lord Proudly proves that this supposition is impossible by questioning, 'Who should go with her, man?'
Weathercock contains a number of references to contemporary events : the dispute over the succession to Juliers
and Cleve (Act I. 2), the gunpowder plot of 1605 (Act I. 2),
the statute by which James I made bigamy a felony (Act

V. 2), the indiscriminate conferring of knighthood by James (Act I. 2), the plague (Act II. 1). Several plays of the day are mentioned either by name or indirectly. As we have seen, Lord Feesimple mentions *Long Meg* and the *Ship*. The title of one of Jonson's plays is incorporated in Abraham Ninny's remark, 'Here's one knows the case is altered' (*Weathercock*, Act V. 1). There are allusions to Friar Bacon and the brazen head (*Weathercock*, Act V. 2); to Lawrence of Lancashire, a boisterous character in a play by Heywood and Brome (*Weathercock*, Act V. 2); to the pouch of Fortunatus (*Weathercock*, Act III. 2); and to the play:

> .... where the fat knight, hight Oldcastle
> Did tell you truly what his honour was.
>
> *Amends*, Act IV. 3.

In *Weathercock* there are two quotations from the *Spanish Tragedy* and two other references to Hieronimo. Although Moll Cut-Purse is a contemporary character, her appearance in *Amends* recalls the *Roaring Girl* of Middleton and Dekker. There appears to be a reference to *Mucedorus* when Lord Feesimple says of his father, 'He looks like the bear in the play; he has killed the lady with his very sight' (*Amends*, Act V. 2). Other literature is spoken of also: the *Mirror of Knighthood* (*Weathercock*, Act IV. 2), Friar Tuck (*Weathercock*, Act V. 2), the Lord of Lorn, the hero of an old ballad (*Amends*, Act III. 4).

Field's plays can lay no claim to modesty; even for a Jacobean he is outspoken. He could scarcely have been among the writers of comedies of manners and escaped coarseness, yet he need not have been so frankly obscene. He seems to enjoy giving a coarse turn to the conversation whenever it is possible, even though the coarseness has no dramatic excuse. His most virtuous women talk among themselves with an open vulgarity. It seems almost as though the young actor were taking advantage of his popularity in seeing how far he could go. No doubt he intentionally catered to the vulgar taste of the lower element of his audience, but it is noticeable that he did so with great gusto! In common with the other dramatists of the decadence, he held the opinion that chastity is found only in women, and then is due to one of two causes: the most plausible excuse for chastity is lack of opportunity to violate it; the only other reason for it is calculating policy. He cannot conceive of a woman that is pure of heart. She is but a 'bauble,' and her affections veer with every amorous breath. The title of his first play shows his attitude. When he dedicates it to 'Any Woman that hath been no Weathercock,' he assumes that he is dedicating it to nobody. The theme of *Weathercock* is stated near the close of the first scene: 'Know'st not how slight a thing woman is?' He states that it 'is impossible to find one good one among them;' they are 'mischiefs' and 'diseases,' and through their craftiness bring mischance to men. Though he is clever to portray woman as a weathercock, he is still more clever to make her an amends without the slightest change in attitude. Field still contends that females are 'deep dissemblers,' and that 'an eel by the tail's held surer than a woman.' Although Lady Bright produces some very good rhetoric on the subject of honor for Bold's edification, she does not despise him for his scheme against her chastity, but declares, 'My blood forsakes my heart now you depart.' Field rails at women, but he does not preach. He believes that a play should be 'a mirror of men's lives and actions,'[8] and simply portrays his conception of woman as a queer species, lending itself especially well to comic treatment. Presentation of the ridiculous lies back of his coarsest scenes. Even in such a scene as that between Wagtail and the page in *Weathercock* (Act II. 1), he is ridiculing the idea of this loose woman's trying to decide upon a suitable person to dub father of her child, so that she can save her

---

[8] *Weathercock,* Address to the Reader.

'honesty.' Field had told Fletcher that he wished to write a play with a 'morality sweet and profitable,' but he does not reward his characters according to their deserts. The wavering Bellafront is ultimately married to her first lover; Wagtail finds a mate not wholly unsuitable in Sir Abraham Ninny; Bold wins the Lady Bright. It is true that Field sometimes lets a scornful tone creep into his satire, but he usually keeps his good humor and is content with showing that vice has a ridiculous side which should make all beware who fear the scourge of laughter.

Although the bitterest shafts of satire are hurled at woman, she is not the only subject of his wit. Her use of cosmetics is ridiculed, and the recipe for a beauty mask is caricatured in Bold's list of ingredients, which is so revolting that Lady Bright exclaims, 'Fogh! no more of thy medicine' (*Amends,* Act III. 3). The stilted language of compliment is laughed at through Pendant; the use of tobacco, through Lord Proudly and others. Interest in pedigree is made extremely amusing by means of Sir Abraham's proud boast that his father is a Ninny and his mother was a Hammer. The self-importance of the newly-created knight is also incorporated in Sir Abraham. As he struts and boasts, we are glad that the fond parents did not spare expense to secure the 'rub-a-dub of knighthood' for the 'forward child.' The corrupt state of law and of religion are major subjects for Field's satire. In presenting the condition of law, he especially attacks the ease with which bribery is used to secure favorable verdicts. Strange refuses to go to law, giving as his reason:

> For some say some men on the back of law
> May ride and rule it like a patient ass,
> And with a golden bridle in the mouth
> Direct it unto anything they please.
>
> *Weathercock,* Act II. 1.

He feels that people will criticise the outcome of the case and will say, 'Your greatness and our money carries it.'

The same idea is brought out in *Amends* (Act IV. 3), when Frank says that Lord Proudly and the nobility:

> Have such a golden snaffle for the jaws
> Of man-devouring Pythagorean law,
> They'll rein her stubborn chaps even to her tail.

The rottenness of the clergy and the hypocrisy of the Puritans are revealed in Field's presentation of both Puritan and Priest. Though Bold has come out of Blackfriars, the great Puritan settlement, and has all the external marks of a good Puritan, his piety is little sounder than that of the Restoration gallants. It is much to Scudmore's surprise that the priest in *Weathercock* (Act II. 1) refuses a bribe; he says:

> I seldom knew't refused yet by thy coat
> But when it would have been a cause of good.

The priest in *Amends* (Act V. 2) even acknowledges that he is 'already undone by wine and tobacco.'

The sprightliness of Field's style is hard to analyze. It is largely a matter of tone and seems to spring from his own aloofness from the story and the characters. He is not sympathetic with these creatures that he portrays and is concerned with their actions rather than their emotions. The characters themselves are very carefree and take both their traits and their affairs in a matter-of-fact way. When Count Frederick finds himself deprived of his rich and beautiful wife, he is not hurt at all; he merely remarks, 'If it be not one of the honestest, friendliest cozenages that e'er I saw, I am no lord,' and proceeds to look about him for another wife. Pouts has been guilty of defaming Kate; but when Strange brings him in, she only calls out casually, 'O sister, here's the villain slandered me,' and her husband makes a pun! The dialogue is light, quick, and conversational, used to carry forward the story instead of to reveal character. The longer speeches are rhetorical and afford an opportunity for the display of histrionic talent. The more solid thoughts are compressed into the scope of an aphorism.

In fact, Field abounds in pungent phrases which are temptingly quotable: 'Honour is honour, but it is no money;' 'Make not a wound with searching, where was none;' 'No man's judgment sits in justice's place;' and so we might continue for pages from either play.

Closely related to this buoyancy of spirit of Field's is a careless haste in writing which reveals indifference to details. This carelessness occurs most noticeably in his broken lines and rough, changing metre. The lines are often so divided between speakers that it is very difficult to tell whether the speeches should be taken together as forming one line, or should be considered as separate short lines. The lines are very unequal in length, and vary from three to six feet. The irregularity in metre often causes the verse to be very rough. It is necessary to do violence to the pronunciation of words in order to scan the line; often it is essential to slur several syllables. Stressed syllables at the opening of the line are found, and are compensated for by following anapests. Examples such as those below may be chosen at random from either play;

> *Sir J. Wor.* Captain, I could have been contented well,
> You should have married Kate.
> *Kate.* So could not Kate.
> *Sir J. Wor.* You have an honourable title.
> A soldier is a very honourable title:
> A captain is a commander of soldiers;
> But look you, captain; captains have no money;
> Therefore the Worldlys must not match with captains.
> *Pouts.* So, sir, so.
> *Sir J. Wor.* There are brave wars.
> *Pouts.* Where?
> *Sir J. Wor.* Find them out, brave captain.
> Win honour and get money; by that time
> I'll get a daughter for my noble captain.
> *Pouts.* Good, sir, good.
> *Sir J. Wor.* Honour is honour, but it is no money.

> *Weathercock*, Act I. 2.

> *Ingen.* I love her better than thy parents did,
> Which is beyond a brother.
> *L. Proud.* Slave! thou liest.
> *Ingen.* Zounds!
> *Frank.* Kill him!
> *L. Hon.* O, hold! Sir, you dishonour much your brother
> To counsel him 'gainst hospitality
> To strike in his own house.
> *Ingen.* You, lord insolent, I will fight with you:
> Take this as a challenge, and set your time.
> *L. Proud.* To-morrow morning, Ingen;
> 'Tis that I covet, and provoke thee for.
> *Frank.* Will you not strike him now?
> *Ingen.* No; my good boy
> Is both discreet and just in his advice,
> Thy glories are to last but for a day:
> Give me thy hand;
> Tomorrow morning thou shalt be no lord.

Vivacity is also shown in the omission of words: 'I not desire it, sir,' 'Will cause it vanish,' or 'Spite of mine approved integrity.' There is a striking confusion of pronouns: *you, thou,* and *ye* occur indiscriminately in all cases:

> Why, Captain, though *ye* be a man of war, *you* cannot subdue affection.
>
> *Weathercock,* Act I. 2.

> *Ye* fillers of the world with bastardy,
> Worse than the diseases *ye* are subject to,
> Know, I do hate *you* all: will write against *you,*
> And fight against *you.*
>
> *Weathercock,* Act II. 1.

> Fie, servant! *You* show small civility
> And less humanity; *d'ye* requite
> My husband's love thus ill? for what *d'ye* think
> Of me, that *you* will utter to my face. . . . .
>
> *Amends,* Act II. 3.

In his effort to give to the audience information that has been previously overlooked, Field drags in very awkward parenthetical exposition or an explanatory aside, instead of revising what has already been written. At the end of the first act of *Weathercock* Neville and Scudmore rush from the stage to try to check Bellafront's marriage but make no plans. When Neville appears at the opening of the second act, he explains his disguise and adds:

> By this means, when my friend confronts the maid
> At the church door (where I appointed him
> To meet him like myself; for this strange shape
> He is altogether unwitting of),
> If she (as one vice in that sex alone
> Were a great virtue) to inconstancy past
> Join impudency, etc.

Lady Honour pretends to acquiesce in her brother's wishes but explains to the audience, 'I must do this, else they had fought again' (*Amends*, Act IV. 3); after telling Sir John that his wife is false, Subtle offers to bring in the wife that Sir John may be an 'ear-witness,' but remarks in an aside, 'I know he will not stay' (*Amends*, Act V. 1). It is such careless habits as the above which help to distinguish Field's hand in unsigned work which may be his.

In his figurative language Field likes to endue breath, looks, and words with a vast amount of vitality. Breath is a *whirlwind, thunder,* or *battery,* according to its volume. If looks do not kill they are at least dangerous, for they fight *stern battles* in the face. Words *knock* at the heart, *shoot* through it, and *cleave* it in twain, or missing the mark, '*pierce* the entrails.' Many of the figures are from animal life, but they are neither illuminating in themselves nor penetrating in their origin. If some one else does not discover that a man is an ass, he confesses it himself. Sir Innocent Ninny, however, is too small for an ass, and so is an 'old dried neat's tongue' and an 'eel-skin.' In spite of these facts his son, Abraham, is a sheep before love transforms him into a lion. People on the whole act like dogs, and two of the characters present an opportunity for a 'fine brace of beagles.' Women have the qualities of

monkeys and crocodiles; we are warned to live 'like a
chameleon,' not like a mole; Pouts has a 'cat-a-mountain face;'
Count Frederick is like a snake in that he casts a suit every
quarter. Some of Field's figures are wholly repulsive:
love is sometimes like a 'dog shut out at midnight,' and
again like 'beef in summer;' an 'ill tale unuttered is like a
maggot in a nut;' the bride is said to need as much dressing as tripe. If people are not animals, they are *jewels,*
and the *lapidary* is called in. The human body is made by
Nature's pattern; sometimes this pattern is lost, and in the
instance of Scudmore, even the gods could never 'make such
another piece as Scudmore is' (*Weathercock,* Act I. 1).
Frequently the body is spoken of as a case which encloses
the spirit. As Bellafront well illustrates, the fair body for
which nature has taken the trouble to invent a pattern sometimes contains a false heart. Field is inclined to hyperbole
and bombast. Bellafront's protestations of love in *Weathercock* (Act I. 1) are especially violent:

> Sooner the masculine element of fire
> Shall flame his pyramids down to earth;
> Sooner her mountains shall swell up to Heaven,
> Or softest April showers quench fires in hell:
> Sooner shall stars from this circumference
> Drop like false fiery exhalation,
> Than I be false to vows made unto thee.

It is difficult to escape drowning: if one successfully avoids
drowning in 'passion and grief,' he is overcome in the
'rivers' of the eyes, or in the 'ocean of love.' The least that
can be expected is to be 'laved in a bath of contrite virginal
tears.' Those that are spared inundation suggest that 'like
the sea, for healths let's drink whole floods.' The nature
figures are very obvious and trite. One may be as cold
as a 'rock of ice,' or mourn for her love 'like to a turtle that
hath lost her mate.' Reputation is sometimes as 'clear as
springs.' The sound of weeping is like the 'murmur of a
silvery brook.' The only rare figure that Field uses is the

comparison of Scudmore's secret to 'fairies treasure' which will vanish if revealed.

His classical training doubtless accounts for his many references to the gods and goddesses and for his allusions to mythology. No play of the period could escape without a 'by Cupid,' but Field's plays run through the whole list of Olympians. Jove with his love escapades is a favorite, for he can readily be used to illustrate many of the points in Field's story. Such mythological characters as Orpheus, Narcissus, and the Gemini are mentioned. Tarquin is used to illustrate ravishment; Hector is referred to; and 'like the fall of Troy' is a popular simile. Even the low characters have knowledge of mythology. We might say of Field as the Page does of Pendant, 'there's all his reading.' Field's study of Latin also affects his phrasing and word order. In the dedication to *Weathercock* he notes the fact, 'and so I end my epistle without a Latin sentence,' as if this were a very remarkable performance for him. Latin words and phrases and occasional quotations do occur in his writing. Idioms such as 'It remembered me' seem due to the influence of Latin. He is fond of the absolute construction and uses it to crowd together facts even when the construction seems awkward as in the example below:

> . . . . a bull
> Being baiting on the green for the swain's sport,
> She walking toward it, the vexed savage beast
> Ceased bellowing.
>
> > *Weathercock,* Act I. 1.

Field's career as an actor gave him a first-hand acquaintance with the taste of his audience and a practical knowledge of stagecraft. He had been on the stage nine years when he wrote his first play and knew that many of the trials of the dramatist were due to the audience. As Dekker expressed it in *Knight's Conjuring,* a dramatist is one who 'workes but like Ocnus, that makes ropes in Hell; for

as hee twists, an asse stands by and bites them in sunder,
and that asse is no other than the audience with hard hands.[9]
In order to avoid the disapproval of the audience, Field
tried to give them what they liked, both in theme and in
staging. The Elizabethan audience was especially fond of
spectacle. He caters to this love when he stages the wedding processional in both plays and concludes *Weathercock*
with an elaborate masque, which brings every character
on the stage and features the hero and heroine leading a
costume dance. He did not overlook the important place
of music in making a play attractive. At the end of the
first act of *Weathercock,* 'music plays' as a signal that the
bride is ready, and Count Frederick orders, 'Put spirit in
your fingers! louder still, and the vast air with your enchant-
ments fill.' When the wedding party approaches the church,
there is music again, and a boy sings to the 'tuned music,'
after which the cornets play. There is loud music when
the party comes from the church. During the masque there
is, of course, music and dancing. The play ends with the
direction given by Sir John Worldly: 'On, parson, on; and,
boy, outvoice the music.' The story of *Amends* does not
lend itself so well to the introduction of music, but there
is a pleasing serenade at one o'clock at night (*Amends,* Act
IV. 1). Closely allied to the pleasure in spectacle is the
delight which the crowds took in witnessing fights and
rowdy scenes. In *Weathercock* Strange and Pouts fight
with swords on Lambeth Field; Mistress Wagtail pulls out
a knife and offers to stab herself; Bellafront displays the
knife hanging at her side ready for use, but since she post-
pones stabbing herself until after the evening's festivities,
she is spared. *Amends for Ladies* has more scenes of this
nature. In Act I. 1, Welltried draws his sword, and Lord
Feesimple swoons at the sight. In Act III. 2, Ingen almost
falls upon his sword in grief over Lady Honour's disap-

---

[9] Thomas Dekker, *Knight's Conjuring* (London, 1841), pp. 76-7.

pearance, but being promised death on the morrow by Lord Proudly, he waits and in Act V. 3 meets Lord Proudly for a duel. Here Lady Honour, disguised as a page, and Lord Proudly both are slightly wounded, and the audience has the pleasure of seeing a little blood flow. The lower classes were probably delighted most of all with the tavern scene, Act III. 4, where oaths and swords fly with equal rapidity, and pots and stools are hurled through the air. After the violence of this scene the audience is gradually let down by the appearance of Lady Bright brandishing her sword at Bold and threatening to kill either him or herself as necessity demands, and by Ingen's dramatic defense of his stolen marriage as he stands armed 'with his sword in his hand and his pistol.' Field likes to excite his audience to a high pitch and then suddenly avert disaster, as in the duel scene between Lord Proudly and Ingen. Just as the duel is becoming interesting, Lady Honour rushes in and puts a stop to the fighting by revealing her identity.

The amusement of the spectators is further provided for by the frequent appearance of the comic characters. In *Weathercock* the comic characters are introduced in the second scene, and at least two of them appear in eight of the remaining ten scenes. Although the plot of *Amends* is more serious in nature and in itself holds the attention, six of the fourteen scenes have comic characters present on the stage. The source of our mirth at these characters is largely external; they are neither witty in themselves nor the cause of wit in others. They amuse us by their dress, mannerisms, tricks, and word-play.

The dialogue shows that Field realized that both actor and audience found pleasure in quick repartee. Except where exposition makes greater length necessary, the speeches are remarkably short. In *Weathercock* almost half of the speeches are only a line or less in length; fifteen of the speeches are just a single word, usually an exclamation. In *Amends* more than one-third of the speeches are limited to a single line. Speech in unison is one of his devices for enlivening the stage. In each play there are some thirteen cases where all the characters speak in chorus style, besides numerous duets, trios, and so on. The frequency with which he uses pithy sayings is partly due, no doubt, to his knowledge that they gave mental pleasure because they could so easily be remembered and carried away by the audience. Many of the speeches have no other purpose than to provoke mirth. Such are touches like this:

> *Pendant* (to Count Frederick). Then you know nothing that
> is worth the knowing.
> *Pouts.* That's certain: he knows you.

Field's stage directions are remarkable for their completeness; and since Field was acting in the companies that produced his plays, this care for detail evidences his unusual technique. Stage entrances and exits are managed with skill. The audience is warned by those on the stage that another character is coming on, or they call the name of the entering character and give some clue as to his relation to those already known to the audience. The wedding guests are assembling at Sir John Worldly's, and the spectators are kept informed as to who the different arrivals are:

> *Count F.* Here's more guests.
> *Pouts.* Is that man and wife?
> *Pen.* It is Sir Innocent Ninny: that's his lady,
> And that Sir Abraham, their only son.

Lady Bright is discussing her suitor with her friends; suddenly one of them announces, 'Peace, here's the man you name.' The stage directions not only indicate the action which is to take place, but frequently stipulate the mood of the character. It seems as though Field had his attention fixed on what was to take place on the stage, and on how the characters were to appear, rather than on the creation of character. The kind of thing that he does is well illustrated by the following directions from *Weathercock,* Act II. 1:

> Music. Enter Sir John Worldly, who meets the parson, and entertains him; Count Frederick, Bellafront, Strange, Katherine, Lucida with willow; Pendant, Sir Innocent Ninny, Lady Ninny, Mistress Wagtail, Sir Abraham melancholy. The Wedding Party walk gravely before all. Scudmore stands before them, and a Boy sings to the tuned music.

Directions circumscribing the action are very complete for early seventeenth century: 'Seldom, having fetched a candle, walks off to the other end of the shop. Lord Proudly sits by Grace' (*Amends,* Act II. 1). Additional suggestions as to what the characters are to do upon the stage are given within the lines. Neville says to Scudmore (*Weathercock,* Act I. 1):

> O, Prythee, run not thus into the streets!
> Come dress you better: so. . . . . .

A character never has to walk off the stage without some reason's being indicated. At the close of Act III in *Weathercock,* Field has to get five people off the stage: Abraham and Pendant announce that they are going to overhear Mistress Wagtail 'venting her moan;' Captain Pouts sends his servant to 'bespeak supper at the Bear;' Strange says to Pouts, 'I'll tell you more: let's walk,' and so the stage is vacated. A noticeable device for giving cues is the employment in one speech of a phrase that is repeated at the beginning of the following speech, as in *Weathercock,* Act III. 2:

> *Bellafront.* For God's sake, do not speak a word more to me.
> *Scudmore.* Not speak! Yes woman, I will roar aloud.

It is difficult to point out marked peculiarities in a writer's vocabulary. Perhaps the most noticeable thing about Field's word-usage is his employment of obvious Latinisms and other somewhat unusual forms of expression: *corrival;* *exquire* the truth; the 'company *convented* there;' to '*expire* breath;' to *respire;* to '*respite* woe.' He often uses intransitive verbs in a transitive sense: '*surcease* our love;' to '*participate* affairs;' to '*philosophise* his spirit.' Adverbs are given an incorrect comparative in *ier: safelier, cleanlier.* *Robustious* and *torturous* are used as adjectives; *burthenous* is employed for *burdensome; suspect* is used for *suspicion;* 'she and her honour *are precipitated;*' one is warned to be *cautelous* 'not to wound my integrity;' knowledge is *practic;* a *gallimaufry* may be made in the blood; the gallants are described as *frumping;* one used as a tool is called an *engineer.* Over and over again appear nouns ending in an extra *y: innocency, continency, impudency, inconveniency,* and so on. He is partial to the word *white* in the sense of innocent: *white* hand, '*white* original creation,' *white* soul, *whiter* virgin. The words *chaste* and *chastity, innocent, innocence, innocency* recur more frequently than any other important words, in spite of the fact that Field seems to have had only a lexical acquaintance with them. Other words often ' repeated are: *surfeit, forfeit, counterfeit, scurvy, scurvily, doat, basilisk, mischief* (in the sense of misfortune), and *diseases.* He assembles a whole anthology of oaths. *'Sheart* and *Heart, 'Swounds* and *'Zoons,* and *'Sfoot* are among his major oaths; *i'faith, in troth, by Heaven,* and *pox* are even more prevalent. When oaths fail, *pish, fie,* or *hey-day* fill the gap. *O* completes the mosaic, being used thirty-seven times in one play and thirty-six in the other. Whether from haste or carelessness in writing, or from personal habit of speech, Field uses many decapitated words. The most frequent of these are: *'cause* for *because, 'fore* for *before, 'ware* for *beware, 'gainst* for *against, 'scape* for *escape,* and *'twixt* for *betwixt. 'Em* is so constantly used for *them* that its presence helps to indicate Field's writing in collaborative work: in *Weathercock* it appears more than twice as often as *them;* in *Amends* it

occurs one and one-third times more than *them*. He is
extremely fond of contractions, notably *ha'* and *d'ye*.

The metrical structure of Field's verse is much like
Beaumont's: the number of run-on lines exceeds the number
of double endings, rhyme occurs frequently, and prose freely
intersperses verse. *Weathercock* has 14.4% double endings,
17% run-on lines, and 8% rhyme; *Amends* has 15.8%
double endings, 24.6% run-on lines, and 3.8% rhyme.
Although Field purports to write in verse, with the exception of the low-comedy scenes, lines of prose are so inter-
mingled with verse that it is often difficult to tell just where
one ends and the other begins. The following lines from
Weathercock, Act I. 2, illustrate the easy interchange of
verse and prose:

> *Abra.* Sweet Mistress Luce, let you and I withdraw:
>   This is his humour. Send for the Constable!
> *Pouts.* Sirrah, I'll beat you with a pudding on the 'Change.
> *Strange.* Thou dar'st as well kiss the wide-mouthed cannon
>   At his discharging, as perform as much
>   As thou dar'st speak; for, soldier, you shall know,
>   Some can use swords, that wear 'em not for show.
> *Kate.* Why, Captain, though ye be a man of war, you cannot
> subdue affection. You have no alacrity in your eye, etc.

Some of Field's verse is of much better quality. The song
in *Amends*, 'Rise, lady mistress, rise,' shows his ability to
write a very graceful lyric. He sometimes writes serious
lines that have a rather stately quality:

> O thou, whose words and actions seemed to me
> As innocent as this smooth sleep which hath
> Locked up thy powers! Would thou had'st slept, when first
> Thou sent'st and profferedst me beauty and love!
> I had been ignorant then of such a loss.

> *Weathercock,* Act III. 1.

The type of play in which Field had taken part as a boy-
actor naturally influenced him tremendously when he began

to write. Nairn attributes to the influence of boy-actors the 'choice of satiric, farcical, or allegorical subjects, where a nimble wit and fancy were needed in the actor rather than the strong passions.'[10] Heywood explains the large amount of satire in the plays for the Children by saying that the playwrights supposed 'their juniority to be a priviledge for any rayling, be it never so violent.'[11] The child-actors also partially explain the fact that the plays given at the Black-friars were so full of songs, instrumental music, and dancing.[12] It was very natural, then, for Field to write satire and to introduce the element of music into his plays, for he had grown up with the idea that a successful play must contain both.

Ben Jonson stands foremost among the individual dramatists who influenced Field. Field belonged to that small group closely knit to Jonson by the affectionate relationship of 'son.' Anyone who had read Latin with Jonson, had seen him write his plays, and had helped to put them on the stage could not have failed to be partly molded by that dominating personality. Field had been in this close personal contact with Jonson as friend and promising young actor in the production of four of Jonson's plays before he decided to try to write plays. In his complimentary verses prefixed to the *Faithful Shepherdess,* it is Jonson, I think, to whom Field refers as the one that shall be his master:

> O opinion, that great foole, makes fooles of all,
> And (once) I feard her till I met a minde
> Whose grave instruction philosophical,
> Toss'd it like dust upon a March strong winde,
> He shall for ever my example be,
> And his embraced doctrine grow in me.

[10] J. A. Nairn, 'Boy Actors under the Tudors and Stuarts,' *Transactions of the Royal Society of Literature* 32. 77 (1914); H. N. Hillebrand, *The Child Actors* 268-70 (1926).

[11] T. Heywood, *Apology for Actors* (Reprinted for the Shakespeare Society, London, 1841) 3. 61.

[12] Wallace, *The Children of the Revels at Blackfriars*, pp. 114-23.

Certainly the doctrine of unities so carefully observed by Jonson grew in Field. He follows unity of place in the Jonsonian sense of confining the scene to one city, and strictly observes unity of time in both plays. In *Weathercock* he even calls our attention to the time element of the play:

> Ne'er was so much (what cannot heavenly powers)
> Done and undone and done in twelve short hours.

There is no doubt that Field is following Jonson in the type of plot that he selected. Like Jonson he is fond of intricate plots and of using tricks for their solution. Field, however, was not a perfect follower of Jonson in dramatic structure. No matter how complicated the structure became, Jonson usually had one main story to which he held throughout. With Field the complication is gained by substituting several stories which are of almost equal interest. Especially is this true of *Amends* in which the stories involving Lady Perfect, Lady Honour, and Lady Bright divide our interest almost equally. His skilful manipulation of these plots in order to gain clearness is directly derived from the study of Jonson's dramatic structure. I have already cited Field's preparation for oncoming events and his explanation of disguise as two of the means by which he keeps the story clear. He is also like Jonson in his clever use of expository soliloquy and in his employment of dialogue for laying the plans for the tricks. His method of introducing a character to the audience is another bit of technique with which Field had become familiar through his acquaintance with Jonson's plays. The device is used so frequently by Field, in fact, that it becomes fairly wooden and loses some of its effectiveness. Sometimes our attention is called to the *humour* which a character represents by the explanation of another character or by personal confession. In *Weathercock* Abraham Ninny makes clear to us why Captain Pouts bears this particular name; Lucida herself tells us that wearing willow is her humour.

Jonson's influence is most readily seen through Field's use of humours to designate the characters. As in Jonson's plays it is sometimes a peculiar mannerism by which the character is recognized: in *Weathercock* Lady Ninny drinks from her aqua-vitae bottle, Lucida wears willow, Mistress Wagtail coughs, and Sir Abraham, like Master Matthew, composes verses. The majority of Field's characters, however, are described by their names as are the characters in the *Alchemist:* Pendant is the parasite; Captain Pouts is sullen and revengeful; Sir John Worldly wishes to marry his three daughters to the richest and most prominent men that he can find, for, he says, 'Worldly is my name, worldly must be my deeds.' In *Amends* the tendency to represent character by name is still more marked. Lady Perfect, Lady Honour, and Lady Bright are three constant women; Sir John Love-all is a profligate; Welltried is the faithful friend; Whorebang, Bots, Tearchaps, and Spillblood are roarers; Bold, Subtle, Lord Proudly, and Lord Feesimple are what their names imply. It is only the externals of humour characters that Field has grasped. Jonson works out each character in detail and differentiates one from another, making the plot an outgrowth of the various natures portrayed. Field uses abstractions, differentiating them only in name and mannerism, and determines the type of the character by the idea which he is trying to portray: for example, the three sisters in the first play represent inconstancy; the three leading women in *Amends* represent fidelity. The characters act from objective rather than subjective necessity, and the name of each fits into the rôle that he is to play. Field has even taken over some of Jonson's characters. He seems to have had Master Stephen of *Every Man in His Humour* in mind when he made Captain Pouts. Sir Abraham Ninny is a queer combination of Sir Amorous La-Foole and Master Matthew. Welltried suggests Wellbred, and Subtle is surely a Jonsonian character.

Boyle passes charitable judgment upon actor-playwrights when he says, 'Now the playwrights of the time, those who were also actors, are apt to repeat themselves, and to borrow unconsciously from other writers in whose plays they had acted.'[13] Probably the Jonsonian words and phrases used by Field were repeated unconsciously, but I think that the plot structure and use of humour characters were in conscious imitation. He also clearly derived some of his cleverest situations from Jonson. Doubtless he used them because he had seen that they were pleasing to the audience. With his knowledge of people and his stage-craftsmanship, Field was able to see what Jonson lacked of being a popular playwright and to popularize some of Jonson's ideas. In situation the opening scene of *Weathercock* closely parallels Act I. 4 of *Every Man in His Humour*. Scudmore is in his room dressing when Neville comes in and reads aloud Bellafront's letter. In Jonson's play Bobadill makes ready while Matthew reads aloud from the *Spanish Tragedy*. Jonson uses the scene only for satire on both the *Spanish Tragedy* and courtly fashion, but Field has conceived of a similar scene as an occasion for real dramatic intensity by letting Neville bring news to Scudmore that Bellafront is even then preparing to marry another man. The idea of having quoted verses recognized by one of the characters is also from *Every Man in His Humour*. Master Matthew reads a poem as his own, but Knowell says, 'This is *Hero and Leander;*' Abraham Ninny in *Weathercock* begins to make rhymes about Lucida's hardness of heart, but Kate recognizes the plagiarism and interrupts with 'God-a-Mercy, old Hieronimo!' Field, like Jonson, enjoys ridiculing the *Spanish Tragedy*. He takes the same passage that Pyrgus quotes in the *Poetaster* (Act III. 3), but with lighter touch he makes fun of it by clever parody (*Weathercock,* Act I. 2). His version is:

[13] R. Boyle, 'Beaumont, Fletcher, and Massinger,' *Englische Studien* 5. 74 (1882).

Strange. Ay, but she thinks you an errant noddy.
Abra. Yet she might love me 'cause I am an heir.
Sir J. Wor. Ay, but perhaps she doth not like your ware.
Abra. Yet she might love me in despite of all.
Lucida. Ay, but indeed I cannot love at all.

Like Master Matthew in *Every Man in His Humour* and
Daw in *Epicoene,* Sir Abraham composes verses; but
whereas Jonson's characters only read their verses to us,
Sir Abraham composes his in our presence. Field has here
combined two ideas in order to get better stage-effect: one,
the forcing of verse from a 'hard-bound wit,' is from
Satiromastix; the other, the ridiculous comments of Pendant
upon hearing the lines, is from the scene in the *Poetaster*
(Act I. 2) where Asinius comments on the efforts of Horace.
Field shortened the scene, made the rhymes absolutely silly,
and put the comments into the form of witty asides. Field
improved on the coughing character which Jonson had introduced with the parson in *Epicoene* when he created Mistress
Wagtail and the old Count Feesimple. The scene in which
Sir Abraham boasts of his ridiculous ancestry closely parallels those in which Sir Amorous La-Foole in *Epicoene* and
Cob in *Every Man in His Humour* derive their pedigree.
The idea of having a man disguised as a woman for a trick
marriage and unmasked after the ruse has carried was probably derived from *Epicoene.*[14] After Dauphine has secured
the property of Morose, he takes off Epicoene's peruke and
says, 'You have married a boy.' When Lord Proudly is
about to fight Ingen because of Lady Honour's disappearance, which he attributes to Ingen's marriage, Ingen
'plucks off' Frank's head-tire and shows that he has married
a man. Field improves on this type of scene when he
has the old Count kiss his fiancée and find the beard of his
son. Like Kastril in the *Alchemist* Lord Feesimple is taught
to quarrel. But Field has the 'fleshing' take place on the

[14] But see *Merry Wives*, Act V. 5.

stage in an uproarious tavern scene. In *Every Man in His
Humour* Formal is deprived of his clothes but finds a suit
of armor hanging in the room and borrows it to wear
through the street. Bold not only is driven forth without
his clothes but is discovered before he reaches his lodgings
and has to lie out of his predicament by swearing that he
lost his clothes gambling.

In writing of the use of cosmetics by the women and
tobacco by the men, of pride in pedigree, of the newly-
created knight, of Priest and Puritan, and of the law, Field
is following Jonson in his subjects for satire. His handling
of these subjects, however, is very different. Jonson writes
satire with a serious corrective purpose and often reveals the
bitterness of one who expects more of life than he finds.
Field sparkles lightly and superficially along; though he is
somewhat judicial in his general attitude, he is, on the whole,
content with portraying folly merely for comic purposes.
Moulton classifies satire in two ways: 'the one declares
a thing ridiculous, the other exhibits it in ridiculous disguise.'[15]   This classification distinguishes the satire of Field
from that of Jonson. Field shows his immaturity and lack
of dramatic insight in that he is usually content with declar-
ing a thing ridiculous. Where Jonson creates a lawyer like
Voltore in *Volpone,* Field has some character rail at the
prevalent injustice of the law. It is only occasionally, as in
the case of Sir Abraham Ninny, that Field attains 'ridiculous
disguise' for his satire.

Next to Jonson, Chapman seems to have had the greatest
influence in shaping the output of the youthful Field.
Though there are echoes from the half dozen Chapman plays
in which Field had acted before 1610, the repetition of
phrase is not so striking as the imitation of Chapman's
rhetoric and aphoristic sentences. It has been customary to
give a biographical turn to Field's sentiments toward women,

---

[15] Moulton, *Ancient and Classical Drama* (Oxford, 1890), p. 256.

but the same cynical attitude is found in the plays of Chapman; and we must remember that Field was uttering those sentiments before an appreciative audience during the formative period of his life. Some of Field's remarks concerning women bear a striking resemblance to Chapman's. The *Widow's Tears* alone is full of contemptuous observations about woman's nature: Chapman says, 'Women's truths are weak' (Act IV. 1); and, 'As for women's resolution, I must tell you, the planets, and (as Ptolemy says) the winds have a great stroke in them' (Act II. 4). Field's worst is not more bitter than this: 'Lust, impiety, hell, womanhood itself, add, if you can, one step to this!' It seems probable that Chapman was Field's master in the matter of equipping plays with full stage directions. Chapman's plays have very complete and explicit stage directions. Seeing the added ease and accuracy of staging which such equipment afforded, doubtless gave Field the idea of furnishing plays with detailed instructions for acting. Through his own stage experience, however, Field was able to enlarge upon Chapman's idea.

Although Field had never acted in any of Shakespeare's plays at the time of the production of his individual dramas, it is only natural that their popularity should cause him to think of them as a good source for hints for his own work. Several situations seem to have been taken over from Shakespeare. Field imitated the popular Portia-Nerissa scene in the scene in *Amends* in which Lady Bright passes judgment on her suitors to Princox. In Lady Honour's disguise as a page and in the account which she gives of herself to Ingen, there is resemblance to Julia or to Viola. The following passage is the reverse of the one in *Henry IV*, Part I, where Falstaff tells of the robbery at Gads Hill:

> *Bold.* How many do you think you have slain last night?
> *Lord F.* Why, *five;* I never kill less.
> *Bold.* There were but *four,* my lord, you had best provide yourself and begone; *three* you have slain stark dead.

Throughout Field's plays there are many echoes of the wording of Jonson, Chapman, Shakespeare, and others. I think that these are unconscious repetition by one whose memory was trained to catch and retain the lines of the older dramatists, and do not indicate intentional plagiarism.

Field's comedies form a link in the chain of plays leading toward Restoration drama. Complexity of plotting is the characteristic which became most popular and was developed to the highest point of intricacy. Humour characters were also carried over and recur still later in Sheridan and some of his followers. The epigrammatic utterance became an obsession with the Restoration dramatists, and vivacious dialogue is one of the charms of their plays. The moral tone of Field is much the same as that of these later writers. Woman's 'honour' is a subject for jest by both sexes; and if, by chance, a woman has any virtue, she boasts of the fact until she appears a prude. With the coming of the drama of sensibility, added stress falls upon the idea of man's reclamation by the unassailable virtue of woman. Such a scene is found in *Amends* when Subtle is convinced of Lady Bright's constancy and kneels to beg her pardon. *Woman is a Weathercock* was revived after the Restoration. It was played by the Duke's company at Lincoln Inn Fields, 1667. Downes does not seem to have known the author and puts it in a list with three of Shirley's plays. This led to Waldron's inserting four instead of three before the words 'comedies of Mr. Sherly's,' and so attributing Field's play to Shirley. Downes's entry informs us that after the reopening of the theatre, 'the Company Reviv'd Three Comedies of Mr. Sherly's, viz.:

> *The Grateful Servant*
> *The Witty Fair One*
> *The School of Complements*
> *The Woman's a Weather Cock*

These plays being perfectly Perform'd . . . . . . prov'd

as Beneficial to the Company as several succeeding new plays.'[16]

As we have seen, Field's plays are realistic comedies of manners, showing little originality in situation or character, and full of satire on contemporary life. What then is Field's place in the history of drama? He commands our attention as the product of external circumstances. As an actor he learned playmaking in a practical school. He knew his audience and what scenes pleased them; he knew the charm of music and the pleasure of sprightly dialogue; and he knew stage technique—how to arrange effective scenes, how to group characters on the stage, and how to manage entrances and exits. His plays furnish a unique example of the work of the clever actor-playwright, who is without any real creative genius.

[16] J. Downes, *Roscius Anglicanus* (Fac. Repr. of 1708 ed., London, 1886), p. 27.

CHAPTER V

Field's certified collaborative work is restricted to two plays: *The Jeweller of Amsterdam, or the Hague,* and *The Fatal Dowry.* The former, which is not extant, was entered in the *Stationers' Register* on April 8, 1654, as written by John Fletcher, Nathan Field, and Philip Massinger. It was based on the murder of the jeweler, John de Wely, at the Hague. This murder occurred in 1616, and, as in the case of *Barnavelt,* the play must have been written shortly after the event. If we had this play, we could more definitely trace the developing dramatic power of Field.

The title page of *The Fatal Dowry* (published 1632) reads, '*The Fatal Dowry:* a Tragedy: As it hath been often Acted at the Private House in Blackfriars, by his Majesties Servants. Written by P. M. and N. F.' These initials undoubtedly stand for Philip Massinger and Nathan Field. The exact date of this play cannot be definitely fixed, but very likely it contains Field's last writing for the stage. Since it was acted by the King's Men, it seems probable that it was written during Field's association with that company, which would restrict the date of composition to the years 1617-9. Lacy Lockert[1] fixes the date as 1618-9 by means of parallels between Massinger's individual plays produced about 1620 and Massinger's scenes in *The Fatal Dowry.*

Field's hand can be very definitely traced in *The Fatal Dowry,* for the style of Massinger is sufficiently different from that of Field to enable one to distinguish the line of demarcation. Creizenach calls this play 'the best example of organic collaboration between two poets of whom one inclined

---

[1] Edition of *The Fatal Dowry,* Princeton thesis, 1914.

more towards the pathetic, and the other towards the lively.'[2]
There has been remarkably little difference of opinion among
critics in regard to the respective shares of Massinger and
Field. The earliest attempt in apportioning the work is
that of Monck Mason in his edition of the play. Though
his division is based merely upon personal impression, it
agrees, in the main, with the later more scientific investigation. He says, 'A critical reader will perceive that Rochfort
and Charalois speak a different language in the Second and
Third Acts, from that which they speak in the first and last,
which are undoubtedly Massinger's, as is also Part of the
Fourth Act, but not the whole of it.' In the Gifford edition
of Massinger's works Dr. Ireland attributes the third act to
Massinger but agrees with Mason in regard to Field's composition of the second act and the first scene of the fourth
act. Fleay undertook a more accurate division by means
of metrical tests and upon this new evidence gave Field:
Acts I. 2b (from 'exeunt Officers'); II. 1, 2; III. 1b (after
'exeunt all but Charalois and Romont'); IV. 1; and V. 2,
80-120.[3] Boyle, by means of the same criteria found similar
results. He gives Field Acts II; III. 1b ('Enter Novall jun.,'
line 317); and IV. 1.[4] Cruickshank[5] thinks that it is hard
'to dissect the play satisfactorily,' and gives Massinger some
of the lines which Boyle thought to be Field's. He thinks
that 'there are clear traces of Massinger's style in the part of
II. 2 which follows the prose passage.' He cites Romont's
speech beginning at line 370. He is not willing to recognize
Field's hand in any of the verse that he considers good. He

[2] Cécile Hugon, *The English Drama in the Age of Shakespeare.*
Translated from 'Geschichte des neueren Dramas' of Wilhelm
Creizenach, p. 68.
[3] F. G. Fleay, *A Biographical Chronicle of the English Drama,
1559-1642* (London, 1891), 1. 208.
[4] R. Boyle, *Englische Studien* (1882) 5. 94.
[5] A. H. Cruickshank, *Philip Massinger* (Oxford, 1920), Appendix
XI, pp. 200-1.

says, 'It is probable that Field wrote the prose scenes in the
play, and possibly the songs; nor would I deny that the
regular ten-syllable blank verse of such passages as Act
II. 2, 178-187 . . . and Act II. 2, 318-328 . . . is Field's
work.' He does not feel that the latter part of Act III
is 'wholly due to Field' and assigns to Massinger lines 438-
78, though he says, 'The ugly line, 464, is not in his
style' and grants that the rhymed couplet (375-6) is
Field's! In regard to Act IV. 1, he thinks the page
undoubtedly Field's, but says, 'Pontalier's speech in the same
scene (119-140) reads to me like Massinger.' Lacy Lockert, in his doctoral thesis of 1914, assigns to Field: Act II;
the latter fourth of Act III; and Act IV. 1.[6]

Broadly speaking, Acts II, III. 1b, and IV. 1, are attributed to Field. There can be no question, I think, of Field's
authorship of this part of the play. Even a cursory reading
results in practically this division, for the above scenes are
full of the characteristics of Field and march along with a
vigor and buoyancy which enable one to point out, almost
without pause, the sections in which he took up the writing.

The most noticeable difference between these scenes and
Massinger's is the difference in tone. In general, there is
a lightness and superficiality in Field's work that enable
one to recognize it with a degree of ease. The story moves
quickly, and as one event follows another, we can almost
see the playwright give the audience the wink. The dialogue is conversational, and even when in verse, it is hardly
distinguishable from prose. There are more humor, repartee,
and word-play when Field is writing, except when he
becomes serious, in which case he waxes rhetorical. Mason

---

[6] E. H. C. Oliphant, *The Plays of Beaumont and Fletcher* (Yale
University Press, 1927), p. 79 (note), gives a much more compli-
cated divison of the play, attributing to Field: Acts I. 1c, 2b (from
'I have begun well' to 'Provided these consent'), II. 1, 2a, c, III. c
(last thirty speeches), IV. 1, 4, V. 1b (Liladam's second-last speech).
He also sees 'joint work' in some other lines.

was right when he felt that the characters speak a different language when Field is writing.

Metrical tests support the claim for Field's authorship of the sections pointed out above. From Boyle's table (*E. S.* V, p. 94) we find 18% double endings, 20% run-on-lines, and 9% rhyme for Act II. 1; 19% double endings, 26% run-on-lines, and 5% rhyme for Act II. 2; 17% double endings, 27% run-on-lines, and 4% rhyme for Act III. 1b; and 19% double endings, 23% run-on-lines, and 6.8% rhyme for Act IV. 1. In his share of this play Field averages 18% double endings, 25% run-on-lines, and 6% rhyme. This is in marked contrast to the 35% double endings, 37% run-on-lines, and 2% rhyme in the remainder of the play. Here, too, we find that the final important pauses (297) exceed the medial important pauses (267), a characteristic of Field's.

Two lively scenes appear to be repeated from Field's earlier plays. In Act II. 2 Beaumelle discusses marriage with Florimel and Bellapert in much the same manner as that of Lady Honour, Lady Perfect, and Lady Bright in *Amends,* Act I. 1. The sprightly tailor-and-lord scene of Act IV. 1 is almost a replica of Act I. 2 in *Weathercock.*

The attitude toward women is that shown by Field. Beaumelle acknowledges to Novall, 'Thy presence blows round my affections vane.' (Act II. 2, p. 126.)[7] In this indication of inconstancy in women we find the same point of view expressed in the title, *Woman is a Weathercock.* Woman is berated in Field's customary manner at the close of Act III (p. 145):

Woman

How strong art thou! how easily beguiled!
How thou dost rack us by the very horns.

As is usual with Field, there are references to the life of the time. It is a 'partial avaricious age' (Act II. 1, p. 110) in which there is neither honor nor virtue; it is not in the

---

[7] The pagination refers to the *Mermaid* edition.

'fashion' to 'meet love and marriage both at once' (Act II.
2, p. 116); the customs of dress are given in Act II. 2, p.
117 and p. 119 and in Act IV. 1, pp. 146-8: the corrupt
state of the church (Act III. 1, p. 139) and law (Act II. 1,
pp. 109-10 and Act II. 2, p. 121) are spoken of with satiric
scorn.

The rhetorical exaggeration strengthens other indications
as to Field's share in the play. Romont feels keenly the
treatment of his friend's father:

> But when I think of the gross injuries,
> The godless wrong done to my general dead,
> I rave indeed, and could eat this Novall;
> A soulless dromedary.
>
> Act II. 2, p. 121.

Later he refuses to tell Charalois of his suspicions of Beaumelle:

> Oh! it will strike disease into your bones,
> Beyond the cure of physic: drink your blood,
> Rob you of all rest, contract your sight,
> Leave you no eyes but to see misery,
> And of your own; nor speech, but to wish thus,
> "Would I had perished in the prison's jaws,
> From whence I was redeemed"—'twill wear you old
> Before you have experience in that art
> That causes your affliction.
>
> Act III. 1, p. 141.

Charalois, doubting the accusation of his wife, reproves his
friend for calling him cold:

> . . . . . Had I just cause,
> Thou know'st I durst pursue such injury
> Through fire, air, water, earth, nay were they all
> Shuffled again to chaos.
>
> Act III. 1, p. 145.

Inability to hold elevation of tone occurs in even the best
passages. The restrained and eloquent funeral oration (Act

II. 1, p. 111) falls into such a line as 'Tears, sighs, and
blacks filling the simile.' The buoyant tone and exuberant
spirit of Field are necessary to account for some passages.
Novall, for example, exclaims against marriage:

> I marry! were there a queen o' the world, not I.
> Wedlock! no; padlock, horselock:—I wear spurs
> To keep it off my heels.
>
> Act IV. 1, p. 148.

It is Field's quickness of wit which we find in the following
bit of repartee:

> *Romont.* So, goodmorrow to your lordship.
> *Novall.* Good devil to your rogueship.
>
> Act II. 2, p. 126.

As in *Weathercock* and *Amends* the opportunity to use
music is not overlooked. The funeral procession (Act
II. 1) enters 'to solemn music;' the second act ends with
music 'playing for the marriage of Charalois with Beaumelle'—a similar conclusion to that of *Weathercock,* Act I,
where music plays for the marriage of Count Frederick and
Bellafront; there are two songs, which sound like Field's
lyrics, the dirge in Act II. 1 and Aymer's song to Beaumelle
in Act II. 2.

The figures of speech are those customary with Field.
The uniting-streams figure is used by Charalois:

> And let these tears, an emblem of our loves,
> Like crystal rivers individually
> Flow into one another, make one source.
>
> Act IV. 1, p. 153.

The tree figure is used several times: Beaumont says of
Charalois, 'Nought but a fair tree could such fruit bear'
(Act II. 1, p. 109); Romont is 'A hearty oak, grew'st close
to this tall pine' (Act II. 1, p. 113); Charalois says,

> My root is earthed, and I, a desolate branch,
> Left scattered in the highway of the world.
>
> Act II. 1, p. 113.

The book figure is used in referring to Charalois, at whom Romont does not wish to have 'men's marginal fingers point' as at a 'lamented story' (Act III. 1, p. 144). A person is spoken of as a cabinet when Beaumelle terms Bellapert the cabinet of her counsels (Act II. 2, p. 115). The references to animals form a large menagerie. The creditors are 'wolvish mongrels,' whose brains should be knocked out 'like dogs in July' (Act II. 1, p. 114); Novall is a 'beast,' an 'elephant,' a 'camel,' a 'soulless dromedary,' an 'ass,' a 'wanton jennet;' he fears that Pontalier would have him be a 'dog.' He and his friends are already termed 'dogs in doublets;' his friends are 'magpies;' Charalois feels a 'wolf' in his breast; Romont is a 'buzzing drone,' and a 'mad ape.' There are several classical references and two allusions to mathematics.

The stage technique indicates that Field wrote these scenes. The funeral procession in Act II. 1 is a splendid piece of pageantry. The dispensing of gifts by Charalois (Act II. 1, p. 113), the discovery of 'a table with money and jewels upon it' (Act II. 2, p. 123), Romont's kicking Novall's followers from the stage (Act IV. 1, p. 151), and Novall's signing the contract under the threat of Romont's pistol—all are effective scenes from the point of view of the audience. Field's portion of the play is equipped with very definite stage directions which carefully circumscribe the action.

The vocabulary is what we should expect in Field's work. Here, as in *Weathercock, exhaust* is used with the unusual meaning of 'draw out.' *Practic* is an odd adjective which Field had previously used in *Amends*. *Gladlier* parallels the adverbial form *safelier* in *Weathercock*. Other words typical of Field are: *innocency, disease, wagtail, gallimaufry,* and the oaths, *'Slid, 'Slight, 'Sdeath, 'Sfoot, Uds-light,* and the exclamations, *humph, ha, pish,* and *i'faith. Hollowly break forth, viperous mother,* and *odiferous fame* are also Field-like expressions. *Ye* occurs in both nominative and objective and is used by both high and low characters.

There are a number of phrasal reminiscences of earlier plays. Both Charalois and Scudmore speak of gold, marble, and jet:

> The golden calf, that was an idol decked
> With marble pillars, jet, and porphyry.
>
> *Fatal Dowry,* Act II. 1, p. 112.

> This is like golden tombs
> Compacted of jet pillars, marble stones.
>
> *Weathercock,* Act III. 2, p. 378.

Novall's greeting to Beaumelle, 'Best day to Nature's curiosity,' (Act II. 2, p. 116) is comparable to Ingen's 'Good morrow to the glory of our age' (*Amends,* Act I. 1, p. 419). Charalois's question, 'Fair Beaumelle, can you love me?' and Beaumelle's answer, 'Yes, my lord,' (Act II. 2, p. 125) have the same ring as Sir John Worldly's 'Kate, do you love him?' and Kate's 'Yes, faith, father.' (*Weathercock,* Act I. 2, p. 354). Pontalier's remark concerning Aymer and Liladam, 'They skip into my lord's cast skins some twice a year,' (Act II. 2, p. 118) is similar to Pendant's statement, 'And then my lord (like a snake) casts a suit every quarter, which I slip into,' (*Weathercock,* Act II. 1, p. 374). Romont's commendation of Novall's early rising, 'So early up and ready before noon,' (Act II. 2, p. 119) reminds us of Neville's 'What, up already Scudmore?' (*Weathercock,* Act I. 1, p. 342). The song (Act II. 2, p. 119) resembles the song in *Amends,* (Act IV. 1, p. 465). The following lines are closely parallel:

> Set, Phoebus, set; a fairer sun doth rise
> From the bright radiance of my mistress eyes!
> * * * * * *
> All want day, till thy beauty rise,
> For the gray morn breaks from thine eyes.

Field's characters are much concerned about the appearance of their clothes. Aymer is disturbed by the disarray which Romont's rough treatment has caused:

Plague on him, how he crumpled our bands.

Act IV. 1, p. 151.

In *Amends* (Act IV. 3, p. 474) Ingen and Lord Proudly are fighting, and Ingen says:

I had liked to have spoiled your cutwork band.

The characters had experienced trouble with their bands in Act II. 2. Pontalier, in replying to the question, 'Dare these men ever fight?' said:

'Oh, no! 'twould spoil their clothes, and put their bands out of order.' (p. 118).

Liladam, in the same scene, calls Novall's attention to his disarray:

Ud's-light! my lord, one of the purls of your band is, without all discipline, fallen out of his rank. (p. 117).

Such an accident had caused great discontent on the part of Master Pert in *Amends* (Act III. 3, p. 455). Lady Bright says:

I have seen him sit discontented a whole play because one of the purls of his band was fallen out of his reach to order again.

Novall, who in Act II. 2, was called 'the map of dressing through all France,'[8] (p. 119), did not usually have difficulty with his clothes:

. . . . his vestaments sit as if they grew upon him, or art had wrought them on the same loom as Nature framed his lordship.

Act IV. 1, p. 147.

Master Pert in *Amends* was of the same type:

I do not think but he lies in a case o' nights.
He walks as if he were made of gins—as if
Nature had wrought him in a frame.

Amends, Act. III. 3, p. 455.

[8] Cf. Beaumelle, Act IV, 1, p. 177, 'the queen of dressing in all Burgundy.'

Aymer goes so far as to call Novall 'Nature's copy that she works form by,' (Act IV. 1, p. 148), and even Romont recognizes that Nature made him (Act II. 2, p. 121). Novall passes the compliment on to Beaumelle:

> This heavenly piece, which Nature having wrought,
> She lost her needle, and did then despair,
> Ever to work so lively and so fair.
>
> Act II. 2, p. 117.

In *Weathercock* Nature's inability to reproduce her work is not that she has lost her needle but that she has fallen in love with her original creation:

> Nature herself, having made you, fell sick
> In love with her own work, and can no more
> Make man so lovely.
>
> Act I. 2, p. 348.

Such perfection caused danger of the lord's falling in love with himself. Aymer begs Novall to put the glass aside:

> Lest thou, dear lord, Narcissus-like, should'st dote
> Upon thyself and die.
>
> Act IV. 1, p. 148.

Count Frederick feared this fate for himself:

> *Count F.*   Pendant, thou'lt make me doat upon myself.
> *Pendant.*   Narcissus, by this hand, had far less cause.
>
> *Weathercock,* Act I. 2, p. 349.

Leaving the matter of nature's copy, we must notice a few other likenesses between this act and Field's individual plays. Romont comes in, bringing 'a battle in his face' (Act IV. 1, p. 150); Strange is in a still worse plight, for looks 'fight stern battles' in his face (*Weathercock,* Act II. 1, p. 367). The phrase 'like a drunken porter' is used by Pontalier (Act IV. 1, p. 149); 'drunk as a porter,' by Abraham Ninny (*Weathercock,* Act III. 2, p. 376). A rather rare figure,

making a comparison with 'fairies' treasure' is used here
as in *Weathercock:*[9]

> ..... 'tis fairies treasure
> Which but revealed, brings on the blabber's ruin.
>
> Act IV. 1, p. 153.
>
> I see you labour with some serious thing,
> And think (like fairy's treasure) to reveal it,
> Will cause it vanish.
>
> *Weathercock,* Act I. 1, p. 344.

The scenes discussed, Act II, Act III. 1b, and Act IV. 1
are easily seen to be Field's, and a study of them in the light
of Field's individual plays only strengthens this apportion-
ment. But there are a few places in which there has been
a difference of opinion as to authorship. Act III has been
the most difficult part of the play to divide. Mason, in his
edition, suggested that it was all Field; Dr. Ireland, in the
Gifford edition, thought that it was all Massinger; Fleay
(*Drama,* 1, p. 208) and Boyle (*E. S.* V, p. 94) tried to
settle the dispute by dividing the act, though they differed
as to the point of division. Boyle marks the beginning of
Field's work at line 317, but Fleay does not recognize Field
until line 345. These twenty-eight lines divide what is Massinger's, with 45% double endings and 36% run-on lines,
from what is evidently Field's, with 17% double endings,
28% run-on lines, and 12 rhymes. Lockert assumes that
both had a hand in this dividing section but points out that
metrical tests indicate Massinger as the author. I think
that a passage of twenty-eight lines is far too short for satisfactory metrical tests, and I see reasons aside from the
consideration of metre for thinking that the passage belongs
to Field. Field, in Act II. 1, had created Pontalier and
Malotin, and in Act II. 2 had added Liladam and Aymer.
Up to this time the remarkable quartet had not appeared in
Massinger's portion of the play. They are continued in

[9] Cf. *Winter's Tale,* Act III. 3, lines 127 ff.

Act IV. 1 by Field. When they do appear under Massinger's hand, it is with a difference. They lack that lightness and directness of speech which is characteristic of them under Field's touch. For example, when Pontalier appears in Act IV. 3, p. 159 as the product of Massinger, he is taking Romont to task for his conduct, and speaks in such an involved sentence as this:

> . . . . I, by your example
> Of thankfulness to the dead general,
> By whom you were raised, have practised to be so
> To my good Lord Novall, by whom I live;
> Whose least disgrace that is or may be offered,
> With all the hazard of my life and fortunes
> I will make good on you, or any man
> That has a hand in't: and, since you allow me
> A gentleman and a soldier, there's no doubt
> You will except against me.

Nothing could be further removed from Field's crisp dialogue. In the disputed lines the characters have that buoyancy and pertness which we expect to find in the characters of this class created by Field. The satire on church preferment, the oaths, *'Sdeath,* and *God's me,* and the word play on *currier* and *curry,* and on *break*—all indicate Field.

Another section in which the authorship has been disputed is the last half of Act I. 2. Boyle thinks that the last 160 lines were 'probably altered by Field.' Fleay gives this section wholly to Field. Except for the fact that there are twelve rhymed lines, I see no indication of Field in this passage. This is a high number of rhymes for Massinger, but 36% double endings and 36% run-on lines support his claim to this section. The diction and tone also point to Massinger; they are not Field's.

Finally, Act V. 2, 80-120 are given to Field by both Boyle and Fleay. Again it is the rhyme, I think, which accounts for this decision. In these forty lines there are six rhymed lines, but there is no other indication of Field's hand to support this clue. The movement is stately, the

sentences are involved, and the diction wholly unlike Field.
I do not think Field capable of the phrase 'blind and slow-
paced justice,' and I am sure that he could never have
produced such a sentence as:

> . . . . . The glory got
> By overthrowing outward enemies,
> Since strength and fortune are main sharers in it,
> We cannot, but by pieces, call our own:
> **But, when we conquer our intestine foes,**
> Our passions bred within us, and of those
> The most rebellious tyrant, powerful love,
> **Our reason suffering us to like no longer**
> Than the fair object, being good, deserves it,
> That's a true victory! which, were great men
> **Ambitious to achieve,** by your example
> Setting no price upon the breach of faith,
> **But loss of life,** 'twould fright adultery
> Out of their families, and make lust appear
> As loathsome to us in the first consent,
> As when 'tis waited on by punishment.
>
> Act V. 2, p. 174.

The two passages in which Field has been seen as collaborator or reviser have, I think, been attributed to him on
insufficient evidence.

While there is no external evidence that Field collaborated
in other plays of the period, the critics have seen his hand
in a number of the dramas of the Beaumont-Fletcher group.
From his individual plays Field is recognized as a dramatist
of a fair degree of ability; and when an unknown hand is
detected in a drama, a simple solution has been to attribute
the work to Field.   In addition to *The Fatal Dowry* there
are nine plays in which various critics have recognized
Field.   These are: *Four Plays in One, The Queen of
Corinth, The Knight of Malta, The Honest Man's Fortune,
The Laws of Candy, Thierry and Theodoret, Bonduca, The
Bloody Brother,* and *The Faithful Friends.*   To read this list
is enough to arouse one's suspicion.   Investigation reveals that
all these attributions have been made on a negative basis—

that is, Beaumont and Fletcher have been studied and their parts positively identified; the residue has been handed over to Field. Fleay goes so far as to say that the very fact of Field's belonging to the King's Men at this time may be taken as evidence that he collaborated in the plays produced. Sykes,[10] and to some extent, Gayley[11] are the only ones who have taken Field's known work as a basis for testing the presence of Field in collaboration. Gayley's study is limited to a consideration of *Four Plays in One.*

Field's work as collaborator with Massinger and Fletcher can be distinguished very readily by means of metrical tests and tricks of style. It is more difficult, however, to tell the work of Field from that of Beaumont, and for this reason it is especially difficult to tell whether Field or Beaumont was collaborating with Fletcher, Massinger, and others in the so-called Beaumont-Fletcher plays. Field seems consciously to have imitated Beaumont, and the more mechanical criteria for detecting authorship are less sure than usual because of the similarity of the work of the two dramatists. Oliphant points out (*E. S.* XIV, p. 166) that the 'two chief distinguishing marks of Beaumont are supposed to be his use of rhyme and his use of prose.' Field, like Beaumont, writes rhyming lines and bits of prose in the midst of blank verse, so that the use of prose and rhyme do not serve as a positive identification of Field. Though the percentage of double endings and run-on lines varies in Field's work from 14.8% double endings and 27.6% run-on lines in his early plays to 18-20% double endings and 20-25% run-on lines in his share of *The Fatal Dowry*, it is in general too near the same as Beaumont's to be a deciding factor. Boyle shows that in *Philaster* Beaumont uses 15% double endings and 26% run-on lines, and that in his later work he averages

[10] H. D. Sykes, *Sidelights on Elizabethan Drama* (Oxford University Press, 1924).

[11] C. M. Gayley, *Beaumont, the Dramatist* (New York, 1914).

10-20% double endings and 20-30% run-on lines.[12] In a number of respects it is almost impossible to distinguish between the work of Beaumont and that of Field. The enclitic *do* is characteristic of both. In their figurative writing both use *rocks, stones, ice* and *snow* in making comparisons. Hyperbole is found frequently in the writing of both. Though less dependent upon the gods than Beaumont's creations, Field's characters call upon the gods in both prosperity and adversity. Gayley notes 'dramatic quotation' as a test for Beaumont, but since Field uses this device at times, it also fails as a means of distinguishing one from the other of these two dramatists. Beaumont often uses the illustration of animals to point out man's superiority on account of his gift of reason. Lady Bright in *Amends* has this point of view, but Field's characters usually overlook the discriminating element and dub each other *ass, elephant, camel.*

How, then, can we determine whether it is Beaumont himself writing in a given play, or Field writing in imitation of Beaumont? Though the problem is difficult, there are some tests which through cumulative evidence seem to me fairly definite distinguishing criteria.

1. Field's number of final important pauses, indicated by period, exclamation point, question mark, dash, colon, and semi-colon, exceed his number of medial important pauses. In *Weathercock* there are 739 final important pauses and only 284 medial important pauses. *Amends* shows 592 final important pauses, and 392 medial important pauses. Field's portion of *The Fatal Dowry* gives less divergence in numbers, but the final important pauses (297) still exceed the medial important pauses (267). An examination of Beaumont's work in *Philaster* and *A King and No King* yields entirely different results. In each case the medial important

[12] R. Boyle, *Transactions of the New Shakespeare Society,* Series I (1880-6), 8-10, p. 581.

pauses exceeded the final important pauses. In *Philaster* I found 508 final important pauses and 526 medial important pauses; in *A King and No King,* 460 final important pauses and 486 medial important pauses.

2. Field, apparently recalling the pleasure of the audience in certain types of scenes, repeats these either from his own work or from the older dramatists. We have already seen that in *The Fatal Dowry* he repeated the tailor-and-lord scene from *Weathercock,* and the scene in which the women discuss marriage and suitors from *Amends.* The latter scene, no doubt, was originally derived from the Portia-Nerissa scene.

3. A part of one paragraph from Gayley is sufficient to make us see the difference between Beaumont's method of characterization and Field's. Beaumont's 'speakers are self-revelatory: expressive of temperament, emotion, reflection. Their utterances are frequently descriptive, picturesquely loitering, rather than, by way of dialogue, framed to further the action alone. And yet, when they will, their conversation is spontaneous, fragmentary and abrupt, intensifying the dramatic situation; not simply as with Fletcher, by giving opportunity for stage business, but by differencing the motive that underlies the action.'[13] Field's characters are never introspective; they do not ponder over their emotions or the reasons for their deeds. They act and act quickly in accordance with the demands of the story and the typical trait which they represent. Their conversation is not used as a chance for poetic utterance on the part of the poet or for analyzing the motives that underlie the action. It is always made the instrument of the plot and is employed to further the story, to explain the action, to *describe* the mood or nature of a character, or merely to amuse the audience. In Beaumont the women characters are marked by innocent helplessness. Beaumont seems to reverence the

---

[13] Gayley, *op. cit.,* p. 290.

innate purity of woman's nature and to have full confidence that chasteness is characteristic of womanhood even in the most distressing situations. Field's attitude is marked by cynicism; he trusts no woman. When a woman protests her chastity for a sufficient length of time, he is willing to admit that she is a marvel in her actions, but he is still unconvinced as to the purity of her heart. Martius is so astonished that Dorigen has stood 'constant and chaste' that he says, 'These wonders do stupefy my senses.' Lady Bright converts Bold from a 'heretic to love and women' and makes him exclaim, 'O widow wonderful.' Beaumont's women accept adversity in love with a commendable spirit of meekness, but Field's women look upon it as a challenge to their ingenuity. With them apparent submission to circumstance is only for the sake of expediency, for they believe that when the crisis comes it will be possible to evade the objectionable situation. Though apparently acquiescing in her brother's demand that she marry the old Count Feesimple, Lady Honour has no intention of giving up Ingen. Just as the ceremony is about to begin, she feigns illness. The physician called in is her lover in disguise to whom she is immediately married by the attending priest. Violante sends word that she will accept Ferdinand as her father wishes, but she plans to tell Ferdinand the real circumstances, knowing that he will then withdraw his suit and leave her free to marry Gerrard. Field's women are outspoken and in their private conversation show their coarseness. In fact, Field gives out gratuitous coarseness on all occasions. With Beaumont the coarseness is imposed by the plot, and we never feel that sort of frank delight in obscenity in which Field indulges.

4. Field, like Jonson rather than Beaumont, often refers to contemporary places and customs of life, to the theatre, and to the corrupt state existing in law and in the church.

5. In spite of the many likenesses in style between Beaumont and Field, there seem to me to be a sufficient number

of differences to enable one to discern Field's work. Beaumont's emotional utterances are sincere and expressive of true feeling; Field's are windy, rhetorical, and unnatural. We never feel that there is real emotion behind Field's rant, and we never find him using that simplicity of expression characteristic of deep feeling, which Beaumont sometimes attains. His characters protest violently, but they do not convince us. The poetic quality of Beaumont's writing is usually lacking in Field. We sometimes feel that he is striving for lyrical beauty, and we occasionally feel that he reaches it, especially in some well-drawn simile, but he cannot hold the tone and spoils the poetic effect by dropping into utterly incongruous lines. Such a break has been noted in one of the famous passages in *The Fatal Dowry:*

> How like a silent stream shaded with night,
> And gliding softly, with our windy sighs,
> Moves the whole frame of this solemnity!
> *Tears, sighs, and blacks filling the simile.*

Act II. 1, p. 110.

Even in the songs, which often have real lyric beauty, the lines fall flat as in the *Dialogue Between a Man and a Woman:*

> Each hair a golden line, each word a hook,
> The more I strive, the more still I am took.

The Fatal Dowry, Act II. 2, p. 119.

Field shows a careless haste in writing which assists one in detecting his hand. He omits words, mixes his figures of speech, and in the effort to make the situation perfectly clear to the audience, drags in exposition parenthetically, or in asides, in a crude manner which often does violence to sentence structure. The abundance of music and the use of song are also typical of Field.

6. The use of figures of speech affords a clue to Field's work. He uses more similes than Beaumont, who usually uses metaphors. Certain figures seem to be favorites with

him. The stream, especially the divided stream converging, is used to depict emotional states; the pine and oak portray the relation between people of different natures; a book or story made by life is used to illustrate the permanency and influence of one's deeds; mathematical references are frequently employed; Nature makes the characters by her pattern; the jewel, or some specific jewel, shows the value of a person; the case or cabinet makes clear the idea that the body is only a receptacle for the spirit; animals of all sorts are seen as counterparts of people; the gods themselves are used to typify certain characters.

7. The stage technique of the actor-playwright is more practical than that of Beaumont. One is never permitted a moment's doubt as to the identity of a character on the stage. The entrances are carefully prepared by the conversation of characters on the stage, and the relation between characters is made clear in the ensuing dialogue. The audience is usually taken into the confidence of the various characters and knows their plots and the disguise used, though it is sometimes given amusement by a fifth-act surprise not an integral part of the main story. The exits are managed so that the breaking up of any group is as natural as in real life. The plays in which Field had a hand are equipped with full and explicit stage directions as well as with many clear indications of the accompanying action within the lines. There are always a large number of scenes which are put in for spectacle or for a definite appeal to the taste of the audience, for Field was concerned with writing a play that would be a popular stage success.

8. The distinctive vocabulary of each dramatist is a fairly safe test. In reading the 'list of 'Stock Words, Phrases, and Figures' which Gayley gives for Beaumont,[14] one is impressed by the great difference between the vocabularies of Beaumont and Field. In a list of some forty-seven

[14] Gayley, *op. cit.*, pp. 282-3.

words, only about a dozen—*basilisk, shoot, print, loathed, mischief, cross, ha, piece, griefs, leprous, venomed*—are found in *Weathercock, Amends,* or Field's share of *The Fatal Dowry.* It is interesting to note that *infect* and its variations, very often used by Beaumont, are not found in Field except once, in *The Fatal Dowry.* Field's most frequently repeated words are: *innocent, innocence,* or *innocency; chaste* and *chastity; continence; white; disease; gyve; surfeit; forfeit; impudence* and *impudency;* and the exclamations, *pish, hum, 'Slight, 'Slid,* and so on. He uses many queer words not found in Beaumont: *blown* as an adjective; *jocundly; antipathous;* to *indue a robe;* to *explicate your thoughts;* to *oppugn an enemy,* etc. One who is the tool of another is an *engine.* Field decapitates words, using *'scape* for *escape, 'ware* for *beware, 'gainst* for *against* and many other like contractions. *'Em* is used for *them* with far greater frequency than with Beaumont. With Field, *'em* greatly exceeds *them;* with Beaumont, *them* is usually employed more often than *'em.* Field continually uses *ye* and *d'ye* in the nominative and *ye* in the accusative with all classes of characters; Beaumont's use of *ye* is very sparing and occurs primarily with the citizen characters in *The Knight of the Burning Pestle.* I have not noticed *d'ye* in Beaumont. Field has a curious habit of employing adjectives as nouns and nouns as verbs. This is not true of Beaumont.

I think that it is possible to distinguish between Beaumont and Field, but I realize that the greatest differences are in the tone and attitude of mind rather than in the more tangible and more easily presented tests of versification. My task, however, is not so much the negative one of showing that certain scenes were not written by Beaumont—in many cases Gayley has adequately shown that Beaumont could not have collaborated in writing the play under question—as the positive one of proving that these scenes were written by Field.

Four Plays has generally been considered as the work of Beaumont and Fletcher. It is ascribed to them by Dyce; Fleay (*Drama* I, pp. 179-80); Boyle (*E. S.* V, p. 81); Bullen (*D. N. B.*); Macaulay (*C. H. L.* VI, p. 144), who says, 'The first two *Triumphs* are probably by Beaumont,' and adds the *Induction;* and Chambers (*E. Stage* III, p. 217 and p. 231). Oliphant (*E. S.* XV, pp. 348-9) sees Field instead of Beaumont in the *Induction* and *Triumph of Honour* but gives the *Triumph of Love* to Beaumont.[15] Gayley (*Beaumont*, pp. 302-3) follows Oliphant in ascribing the *Induction* and *Triumph of Honour* to Field, adds Scenes I, II, and VI of *Triumph of Love* 'on the basis of diction,' and considers the remaining scenes early Beaumont 'revamped by Field,' or Fieldian imitations of Beaumont. Sykes (*S. E. D.,* pp. 205-11) claims the *Induction* and both *Triumphs* for Field on the basis of diction and of parallel passages. His proof, however, rests more heavily on likenesses to the *Queen of Corinth* than on evidence from Field's known plays. I do not see sufficient reason for thinking that two different authors had a hand in the first two *Triumphs,* and I feel that the weight of evidence for authorship is on the side of Field.

One look at the result of the application of metrical tests to the *Four Plays* is sufficient to convince one that there is a division of authorship occurring after the first two *Triumphs*. Evidently, also, the first two *Triumphs* are by the same hand, and the last two by Fletcher, for the *Triumph of Honour* shows 11.3% double endings, 25% run-on lines, and 11% rhyme; the *Triumph of Love*, 15.6% double endings, 25% run-on lines, and 9% rhyme; the *Triumph of Death*, 70.3% double endings, 10.9% run-on lines, and no rhyme; and the *Triumph of Time*, 68% double endings,

---

[15] In his new study of the plays (*op. cit.,* p. 377) he somewhat doubtfully agrees that the *Triumph of Love* is Field's and adds the *Prologue* to the *Triumph of Death.*

12.6% run-on lines, and no rhyme. There are but two candidates for the authorship of the first two *Triumphs,* Beaumont and Field. The metrical tests might be used to support the authorship of either one, but the fact that the final important pauses exceed the medial important pauses indicates Field.[16] The general tone of the writing, the vocabulary, and other evidence also point to Field. I think that the passages which are most like Beaumont are due to Beaumont's influence on Field. The general coarseness of the comedy, the very evident enjoyment in giving the conversation an unnecessarily coarse turn, is like Field. In contrast to this play to the lower element of the audience, we find the unassailable chastity of Dorigen. She is such a figure as Lady Perfect or Lady Bright in *Amends.* When she 'offers to stab herself' in preference to yielding to Martius, Martius kneels converted. This scene seems to combine that of Lady Honour's seizing a sword to convert Bold with that of the repentant Subtle kneeling before Lady Bright. These women stand out as such rare examples of chastity that the men are overcome with remorse for having doubted them. Sophocles implores, 'I prythee kill me,' and Subtle in *Amends* begs, 'I prythee break my head.' The interrupted fight in *Triumph of Honour,* Scene I (pp. 495-6)[17] is reminiscent of the abruptly closed duel in *Amends* (Act IV. 3, p. 474) and in the *Queen of Corinth* (Act IV. 4, p. 468). The discovery of an unknown character who clears up plot entanglements is repeated in the unveiling of the long lost Cornelia (Scene VI, p. 532). The crowd shouts 'Ha!' and Rinaldo exclaims:

---

[16] This is true of each scene in the Triumphs except Scene IV in the *Triumph of Love* where there are two more medial important pauses than final important pauses. The total figures are very convincing: the *Triumph of Honour* has 254 final important pauses and 171 medial important pauses; the *Triumph of Love* has 333 final important pauses and 193 medial important pauses.

[17] All references to pagination in the Beaumont-Fletcher plays are to the Dyce edition.

> By all man's joy, it is Cornelia
> My dearest wife.

The discovery had been used twice very effectively in *Weathercock*. Neville reveals that he has played the rôle of parson, and that Bellafront's marriage is, therefore, not legal. Strange pulls off his soldier's disguise to the following staccato tune:

> *Katherine.* O my dear Strange!
> *Sir J. Worldly.* My son!
> *Scud., Luc., Bel.* Brother!
> *All.* Young Strange!

The exclamations upon recognition are quite exaggerated in the *Triumph of Love* when Ferdinand and Violante awake (Scene VI, pp. 533-4):

> *Rinaldo.* Son!
> *Cornelia.* Daughter!
> *Ferdinand.* Father, mother, brother!
> *Gerrard.* Wife!

But not all Field's characters are thus delighted to have recognition. Frigoso does not wish to recognize Rinaldo (*Induction*, p. 480), for he is 'too punctual a courtier.' This scene is a dramatization of Sir Abraham Ninny's idea that lords are expected to look 'as if we had never seen the party when we meet next' (*Amends*, Act I. 1, p. 423). Nicodemus has a list of attractions (*Triumph of Love*, p. 495) comparable to those of Sir Abraham Ninny (*Weathercock*, Act I. 2, pp. 357-8). He has all the airs and even the oaths of a knight although he is only anticipating knighthood. Ferdinand pleads with Gerrard to keep his own secret just as Neville remonstrates with Scudmore in *Weathercock*. In *Triumph of Love* Violante's drinking the remainder of the poison and the use of the sleeping potion which produces the appearance of death seem reminiscences of *Romeo and Juliet*.

Although the setting is foreign, there are references to contemporary life. The *Induction* opens with an allusion to the immoral practices carried on in the theatres of King James's reign. After the death of the usurping Duke (*Triumph of Love,* Scene III, p. 519), there are many libels, elegies, and epigrams made, as was the custom when a man of prominence died. Nicodemus is the low-class type so frequently knighted after James came to the throne. Two lords get places by the King's chair at the theatre, for 'to be seen in such a position is good security in the sight of creditors' (*Induction,* p. 481).

Besides the references to the theatre in another connection above, there are only two more allusions. It is said to be desirable to have the 'the fencing of our tragedian actors,' and we are told that the 'wretched hangman ends the play.'

The chief subjects for satire are, as is usual with Field, the law, which may be ruled by the great, and the affectations of the courtiers.

These two *Triumphs* are full of rhetorical passages in which exaggeration and protestation take the place of real feeling. In the *Triumph of Honour* Sophocles, in his second speech (Scene I, p. 484) declares:

> But look thee, Martius; not a vein runs here,
> From head to foot, but Sophocles would unseam,
> And, like a spring garden, shoot his scornful blood
> Into their eyes durst come to tread on him.

Dorigen speaks with the vehemence of a true Field character when she says of the gods:

> Know if they dare do so, I dare hate them,
> And will no longer serve 'em.
>
> *Triumph of Honour,* Scene II, p. 503.

Martius quotes Dorigen's vow (*Triumph of Honour,* Scene II, p. 502), 'Sooner these rocks should be remov'd then she should yield.' This is in much the same vein as Bellafront's affirmation, 'Sooner her mountains shall swell up to heaven, than I be false to vows made unto thee' (*Waathercock,* Act I. 1, pp. 341-2).

There are certain turns of expression, a buoyancy, and a
sense of haste which give one the feeling of the presence
of the young actor-playwright, but are hard to classify and
apply as tests of authorship. 'O wretched men!' exclaims
Dorigen, 'with all your valour and your learning, bubbles'
(*Triumph of Honour*, Scene II, p. 504). Valerius pleads
with Martius, 'Martius, draw thy sword, and lop a villain
from the earth' (*Triumph of Honour*, Scene II, p. 500).
Gerrard parts from Violante in a flurry:

> Farewell, my life and soul. Aunt, to your counsel
> I flee for aid. O unexpressible love! thou art
> An undigested heap of mixed extremes,
> Whose pangs are wakings, and whose pleasures dreams.

Triumph of Love, Scene I, p. 511.

When Benvoglio and Randulpho visit Violante, Randulpho
asks:

> How fares my Niece?
> *Viol.* A little better, Uncle, then I was,
>   I thank you.
> *Rand.* Brother, a mere cold.

Triumph of Love, Scene III, p. 521.

Surely no one but Field could make such a comparison as
'like a Dryad out of a wash-bowl,' or 'run like a spout.'
Even when the moment should be deeply emotional, Field
cannot get away from a casual tone. Gerrard has just
revealed to his friend, Ferdinand, that Ferdinand's betrothed
is his own mistress. Ferdinand says, 'What did he say?
Gerrard, whose voice was that?' Gerrard can even make
puns with the waiting woman who brings him news of
Violante's plight after the discovery of her guilt, and Benvoglio turns jovially to the hangman and says, 'Stay, hangman, I have work for you: there's gold, cut off my head,
or hang me, presently' (*Triumph of Love*, Scene VI, p.
533). Sophocles tells Martius that he must die unless he

can successfully defend himself. Martius answers with unconcern:

> Why Sophocles,
> Then, prythee, kill me; I deserve it highly.
> *Triumph of Honour,* Scene II, p. 506.

The song (*Triumph of Honour,* Scene II, p. 503) and the use of even more music than would be expected to accompany such a spectacle as this are what we should expect of Field. Martius, Valerius, and others 'Enter in triumph with Drums, Trumpets, and colors.' 'Solemn music' heralds the approach of Dorigen, and also accompanies the tearing away of the constant stones while Valerius sings. 'Soft music' is played while the bodies of Ferdinand and Violante are brought in.

In both *Triumphs* the handling of the metre is in Field's careless style. The irregularities are almost annoying. There are stressed syllable openings, anapests, and slurred syllables—none of which indicate Beaumont. A few lines, chosen at random, illustrate this point.

Triumph of Honour

1. 'Tis behind yesterday but before tomorrow.
2. But if this jewel hold lustre and value
3. Violate not thy soul too! I have showers
   For thee young man. ....
4. You hurt me, sir! Farewell.—Stay; is this Martius?

Triumph of Love

1. Lest gladness suffocate me? I, I, I, do feel
2. *Benv.*   Say.
   Ang.   She will have the man, and, on recovery,
             Will wholly be dispos'd by you.
   Benv.   That's my wish!

Carelessness is also shown by mixed figures. In the *Induction* Isabella's breast is first a 'crystal brook,' then a 'lovebook clasp'd,' and finally 'frozen water.'

Several of the figures are stock figures with Field. The book figure is one of these. Isabella desires that she shall:

> But be your love-book clasp'd, open'd to none
> But you, nor hold a story but your own.
>
> *Induction,* p. 482.

Reference is made to the 'insatiate Julius' and the 'legend of his deeds' (*Triumph of Honour,* Scene II, pp. 497-8). Benvoglio grieves over Gerrard's act, saying, 'Was thy base pen made to dash out mine honour?' (*Triumph of Love,* Scene IV, p. 524). But when affairs have worked happily, Rinaldo calls for:

> A pen of iron, and a leaf of brass
> To keep this story to eternity.
>
> *Triumph of Love,* Scene VI, p. 535.

Seas and streams, even the ocean itself, are called into service. Isabella is a 'fountain of life' and a 'tributary rivulet;' Emanuel, a 'majestic ocean.' Ferdinand declares that 'neither mountains nor seas shall bar my flight to Vengeance.' Martius admits that his emotion 'Doth ocean-like o'erflow the shallow shore' of virtue. Martius voices the idea that the body is a troublesome repository for the spirit when he begs Sophocles, 'Uncase my soul of this oppressing flesh.' Ferdinand's body is a 'beauteous cloud;' his mind the 'radiant sun.' Dorigen is the only jewel in the play, but has been made by heaven. Ferdinand and Gerrard are the 'parallels of Milan.' The ass, one of Field's favorite norms for comparison, is used four times in these plays. Other animals are referred to: the Captains are 'fish-fac'd;' Florence has an 'ape's face;' Nicodemus has 'eaglet talons,' but is called 'Corporal Cod's-Head;' 'punctilios and punkettos of honour' are not 'worth a louse;' men reading poetry are like bees or spiders, according to what they bear away. There are numerous classical references: Juno, Jove, Mars, Saturn, and Diana are the gods to whom allusion is made; Jupiter's love affairs and Tarquin and Lucrece illustrate the theme;

Fortune's golden ball and an allusion to Ariadne complete the list.

One is impressed by the meticulous care with which the stage directions are given. It is noticeable that the directions are much more brief in the Fletcher *Triumphs* than in the first two. Only once does Fletcher indicate the manner in which the actors shall perform their parts, but Field gives the mood which shall be portrayed: Angelina is 'showing remorse,' the States 'seem sorry,' Randulpho 'in scorn' causes Cornelia to be thrust out 'poorly,' etc. Twice Field uses the device so frequently employed in his plays, that of speech in unison. There are many effective scenes: the preparation of Sophocles and Dorigen for death; Dorigen's offer of herself to Martius and threat to fall upon her sword; the visit to Violante in bed; the drinking of the poison; the waking of Ferdinand and Violante; and, of course, the elaborate dumb shows.

The vocabulary is what we expect from the author of *Weathercock* and *Amends*. The frequent use of *chastity* and *innocence* is characteristic of Field; in these *Triumphs chastity* occurs eight times and *chaste,* four; *innocence* is repeated three times and *innocent,* twice. There are the usual *impudence* and *continence,* and *pish, humph,* and *ha. Beauteous* and *engine, white* simplicity and fairest *white* are familiar expressions of Field's. Such unusual terms as *blown man, couser wale, gyved, miskil, jocundly* (used again in *Queen of Corinth*) and *antipathous* seem to indicate his presence. The phrase, *female tears,* is paralleled in *Amends* by *female hate.* The frequently repeated decapitations: *'gainst, 'fore, 'long,* point to Field. The use of *ye* in both nominative and accusative makes an attribution to Beaumont seem doubtful. *D'ye,* a form not found in Beaumont, occurs, and *'em* is used twice as much as *them.* The indiscriminate use of pronoun forms also helps to establish Field's hand: *you* and *thou,* with corresponding forms for other cases, are used without distinction as to class of person speaking.

We find, for example, such quick changes as: 'Will this content *you?* let him taste *thy* nether lip' (*Triumph of Honour,* Scene I, p. 496); and:

> Now *you* are an ass again;
> For, if *thou* ne'er attain'st, 'tis only 'long
> Of that faint heart of *thine.*
>
> *Triumph of Love,* Scene II, p. 513.

Certain passages in these plays possess a closer connection with Field's earlier work than those cited as an illustration of tone:

> . . . . . the law
> Is but the great man's mule; he rides on it,
> And tramples poorer men under his feet.
>
> *Triumph of Love,* Scene VI, p. 531.

> . . . . Some say some men on the back of law
> May ride and rule it like a patient ass.
>
> *Weathercock,* Act II. 1, p. 369.

> * * * * * *
>
> Sir, Heaven and you have over-charg'd my breast
> With grace beyond my continence; I shall burst.
>
> *Triumph of Love,* Scene II, p. 514.

> . . . to conceal it
> Will burst your breast; 'tis so delicious,
> And so much greater than the continent.
>
> *Weathercock,* Act I. 1, p. 344.

> * * * * * *
>
> . . . . , I am now, methinks,
> Even in the land of ease.
>
> *Triumph of Love,* Scene III, p. 523.

> I was even in Elysium at rest.
>
> *Amends,* Act I. 1, p. 424.

Other passages are closely related to lines in that part of *The Fatal Dowry* which is generally conceded to be Field's:

> . . . my desire's a vane,
> That the least breath from her turns every way.
>
> *Triumph of Honour,* Scene II, p. 498.

Thy presence blows round my affection's vane.

The Fatal Dowry, Act II. 2, p. 126.

* * * * * *

. . . . . thy words
Do fall like rods upon me! but they have
Such silken lines and silver hooks, that I
Am faster snar'd.

Triumph of Honour, Scene II, p. 499.

. . . . . I dare not look.
Each hair a golden line, each word a hook,
The more I strive, the more still I am took.

The Fatal Dowry, Act II. 2, p. 119.

* * * * * *

Thou that didst order this congested heap,
When it was *chaos,* 'twixt thy spacious palms
Forming it to this vast rotundity,
Dissolve it now; *shuffle the elements,*
That no one proper by itself may stand!

Triumph of Honour, Scene III, p. 505.

Had I just cause,
Thou know'st I durst pursue such injury
Through *fire, air, water, earth,* nay were they all
Shuffled again to chaos.

The Fatal Dowry, Act III, 1, p. 145.

Though some of the critics do not attempt to name the
collaborator with Fletcher and Massinger in the *Queen of
Corinth,* four attribute Acts III and IV to Field. Dyce
ventured only 'Fletcher and some contemporary.' Fleay
(*T. S. S.* (1874), p. 60) first favored Middleton, but
later (*E. S.* IX, p. 22) he says this was a mistake in copying.
His final verdict on the authorship (*E. S.* XIII, pp. 34-5
and *Drama* I, pp. 206-7) gives Massinger Acts I. 1, 2, 3b
and V; Fletcher, Acts I. 3a, 4 and II; Field, Acts III and
IV. Boyle (*T. S. S.* (1880-6), p. 609) says, 'perhaps Field
is third.' Oliphant (*E. S.* XVI, pp. 180-1) adds Act V. 3 to
Field's share, except for a few lines attributed to Fletcher.

He divides the play: Massinger, Acts I and V. 1-2, 4; Field, Acts III and IV; Fletcher, Act II; and Fletcher and Field, Act V. 3.[18]   Bullen (*D. N. B.*) does not see Field and divides it: Massinger, Acts I and V; Fletcher, Act II; Middleton and Rowley, Acts III and IV. Macaulay (*C. H. L.* VI, p. 156) attributes the play to Massinger, Fletcher, and a third whom he does not identify. Gayley (*Beaumont, the Dramatist,* p. 237) and Chambers (*E. Stage* III, p. 218) omit it from the collaborative list. Sykes (*S. E. D.,* pp. 211-4) thinks Acts III and IV Field's work.

In regard to Act V. 3, which Oliphant terms 'pure Field with the exception of a few lines which speak themselves Fletcher,' metrical tests are not decisive on account of the brevity of the passage (38 lines); but 32% double endings and 25% run-on lines almost preclude the possibility of Field. These percentages are, however, practically normal for Massinger, and the rhyme-tag at the end of the scene also suggests him. The tone is not unlike Field, but I find no definite indication of his authorship.

Metrical tests do show that the author of Acts III and IV was a different person from the author of Acts I, II, and V. Sixteen per cent double endings and 26.6% run-on lines for Act III and 18% double endings and 26% run-on lines for Act IV are figures which indicate Field's writing at this period (1617, date by allusion to Coryat's *Greeting,* 1616). In Act III the final important pauses exceed the medial important pauses by 73 and in Act IV, by 82.

Several circumstances in Acts III and IV seem to be repeated from Field's earlier work. The foolish 'bought gentry' are used for comedy effects as in *Weathercock.* Onos brags of his pedigree as does Sir Abraham Ninny. He would have us know that he is a 'gentleman on both sides.' The pedigree boast is repeated by a serious character when Euphanes says:

[18] Oliphant retains this division in *The Plays of Beaumont and Fletcher,* p. 399.

> Five fair descents I can derive myself
> From fathers worthy both in arts and arms.
>
> Act III. 1, p. 442.

When Onos feels that his love is hopeless, he throws off his clothes to an accompaniment of impromptu verse (Act III. 1, p. 445), repeating the behavior and some of the ideas of Sir Abraham Ninny when he found himself repulsed by Lucida (*Weathercock*, Act I. 2, p. 359). In Act IV. 4 the duel is interrupted as it was in *Amends*.

As is indicated above, Onos is modeled upon Sir Abraham Ninny, with Tutor and Uncle taking the places of Sir Innocent Ninny and Lady Ninny. Even the legs of Onos are similar to Sir Abraham's: Onos's legs remind one of a crab tree; Sir Abraham's, of a plum tree. The two-faced villain and the sprightly page are typical Field characters. Indeed, the page appears only once after Act IV and then only to make an announcement. The Queen is surely no Beaumont woman; there is no passivity here. She raises Euphanes according to his deserts regardless of public opinion, holds herself a 'competent judge of her own actions,' and when Euphanes is in danger, she leads her troops into the field to protect him. The attitude toward woman reveals Fieldian cynicism. Crates, like Bold in *Amends*, holds that a widow is a 'hungry thing.' The Queen herself thinks of the physical pleasure which might be indulged in with Euphanes and even plays with the idea of marrying him; but, she says, 'Though I love thee, I can subdue myself.' Maids as well as widows are thought of as very passionate creatures and are compared to 'towns afire.' The very manner of characterization denotes Field, not Beaumont. Our fullest knowledge of each character comes from descriptions given by other characters. The characters act and speak solely to advance the plot, or, in the case of the comic characters, to amuse the audience.

There are references to contemporary life and various contemporary manners. In the mention of the 'Ulyssean

traveller that sent home his image riding on an elephant to
the great Mogul' (Act III. 1, p. 439) is an interesting allusion to one account of Coryat's travels published in 1616.
There are two references to customs in the theatre. Merione's room is hung with black like the tragic stage; Onos
is like 'a fellow that I have seen accommodate gentlemen
with tobacco in our theatres' (Act III. 1, p. 438). The
practice of singing ballads about contemporary persons and
events in the drinking houses is mentioned by Euphanes
(Act III. 1, p. 440). There is a slur at the 'fork-carving
traveller,' the 'bought gentry' of King James's reign, and at
the boasts concerning ancestry. The affectations of the
courtier are extensively satirized: his toilet (Act IV. 1, pp.
437 and 455); his 'T beard' (Act IV. 1, p. 454); the signs
of the 'enamour'd courtier' as in *Amends* (Act IV. 1, p.
454); the many excuses for duelling (Act IV. 1, pp. 456-
8); the desire to appear melancholy—a pose of the gallants
(Act IV. 1, pp. 455 and 460); and the conceited phrases
of the gentry.

Beginning with Act III, there is a noticeable difference
in the tone of the play. The movement of the verse quickens,
and the story bounds along. The characters protest in
exaggerated terms, and Crates gives himself up in abandonment to his mood of despair:

> Oh, I could eat my heart, and fling away
> My very soul for anguish: gods nor men
> Should tolerate such disproportion.
>
> Act III. 1, p. 435.

Indeed, he seems anxious to dispose of his life, for later
he threatens to starve in chains or eat his own arms (Act
III. 1, p. 443). But protestation is not characteristic of
Crates alone. Euphanes feels his gratitude so keenly that
he indulges in rhetorical flights:

> .... Whate'er he be
> Can with unthankfulness assoil me, let him
> Dig out mine eyes, and sing my name in verse,

> In ballad verse, at every drinking house,
> And no man be so charitable to lend me
> A dog to guide my steps.
>
> Act III. 1, p. 440.

In Act III the presence and tone of the songs certainly point to Field (see parallel passages). The many cases of careless omission of words are characteristic of Field:

> And I in gratitude was bound to this,
> And am to much more.
>
> Act III. 1, p. 440.

> And what I meant your brother, you obtain'd
> Unto the forfeiter again.
>
> Act III. 1, p. 442.

Some of the figures of speech become almost hopelessly confused. Euphanes, for example, first has wings like Icarus, then 'spreads like a river,' and finally, is threatened with having his roots rended (Act III. 1, p. 436). In the next act he is a mushroom that sits brooding beneath the wings of the Queen! Other figures show Field's tendency to use the first idea that comes to mind without consideration of the question of appropriateness. He speaks of *unscrewing* a mother's love to her son (Act III. 1, p. 445) and makes an elaborate comparison of a brother to an 'eye, ear, arm, and leg' (Act IV. 1, p. 469). Compressed and crude exposition is thrown in parenthetically no matter what violence it does to the grammatical structure of the sentence. In Act III. 1, p. 437, we find this construction:

> Conon's forfeit state
> (Before he travell'd) for a riot he
> Hath from your mother got restore̊ to him.

The Queen questions Euphanes:

> What's the cause my son
> (For my eye's everywhere, and I have heard)
> So violently does thee contumelies
> Past sufferance (I am told), yet you
> Complain not.
>
> Act II. 1, p. 445.

Sudden changes in character are explained in asides. The Queen rails at Euphanes, but in aside says, 'Only to try thee this.' Theanor finds that the Queen resents his telling her that people are making uncomplimentary remarks about her conduct, and to show that his change of tone is policy, not conviction of her innocence, he explains, 'This must not be my way.' All the above evidences of style point very definitely to Field as the author of Acts III and IV.

Field, always fond of using streams, rivers, and torrents in his figurative writing, appears to have been so influenced by the two rivers of Corinth that all things seem watery. 'Violent streams of blood' are 'like Corinth's double torrents.' The love of the people and of the Queen for Euphanes is 'like two floods bearing Euphanes up.' Theanor, however, fears that they will overflow him. He says that Euphanes 'spreads like a river.' Even Euphanes speaks of his own 'blown billows' and calls himself a 'thankful stream.' Corinth seems in danger of becoming inundated, for Agenor and Leonidas plan to 'rush upon the land like Corinth's double torrent' and quench Euphanes (who is now in flames) with 'violent streams of blood.' The book figure and the pine and oak figure recur (see parallel passages). The mathematical figure is used by Crates when he declares to Theanor that he will bend 'one parallel line of love' on his brother, but that 'all lines of love and duty meet in you as in their centre.' The Queen's body is 'a crystal casement 'fore my heart;' Euphanes is a jewel—a pearl; Nature did not make Euphanes in a frame, but picked several flowers from her 'choice banks' to form him as a posy! It is the Queen who has made Euphanes and rejoices 'like a choice workman' that has 'fram'd a masterpiece.' Characters are compared to lions, asses, and elephants, but a little variety is afforded by the introduction of hounds, a lamb, a peacock, an eaglet, and a dove. One discerns Field in this figurative language and in the ten classical allusions used in addition.

The stage technique makes one feel that it is the practical playwright who is writing. Entrances and exits are scrupulously prepared for in the dialogue. Act III. 1 is a noticeably perfect piece of work in this respect. The device of speech in concert is used with excellent effect in three instances. The two acts are crowded with scenes that appear well on the stage. In Act III. 2 the black-hung stage, the candle light, the songs, and the sudden discovery of the fatal ring reveal mastery of stage craft. There are two highly dramatic scenes: Theanor rushes in, kneels before his mother in a manner not unlike Hamlet's, and accuses her of illicit relations with Euphanes; the repentant Agenor and Leonidas give up their swords to Euphanes and, kneeling, beg that the points be turned upon them. Act IV. 4 opens with a dumb show similar to those employed in the two *Triumphs* written by Field, and contains a duel which is broken off by the approach of others—a Fieldian device which yields much excitement to the audience and no harm to the characters!

The recurrence of the different forms of the word *innocent* and of *impudence, chastity, white, surfeit, ginne* and *engine* are corroborative evidence of Field. The exclamations, *pish, humph,* and *ha,* and *'Slight* are constantly used. *'Blown billows'* is an expression that recalls *'blown man'* and *jocundly* and *antipathous* are reminiscences of the *Triumph of Love.* There are several words and word groups that sound like Field: *oraculous, assoile, exquired, occurrents, infantly;* to sit thus *excruciate,* to *insinuate yourself a lodging,* to *retribute his stream.* The adverbial forms, *sweetlier* and *justlier,* and the nouns: *sleeps, helps, mock, blacks, confronts* are Fieldian forms. The decapitations: *'fore, 'gainst, 'less* and *'twixt* are much used; *ye* is found in nominative and accusative; *them* does not occur, but *'em* is found 19 times. Of the 47 words and phrases pointed out by Gayley as belonging peculiarly to Beaumont's vocabulary, I find nine used, but only *cross* repeated.

Some passages in these acts are strikingly like lines found elsewhere in Field. These are, of course, a great help in designating Field's presence. Several similar phrases are on the subject of love. Crates feels that 'love would make a dog howl in rhyme,' but Ingen in *Amends* disdains this 'howling love' and says, ' 'tis like a dog shut out at midnight.' Both Merione and Bellafront are cold; Merione 'sits like a hill of snow;' Bellafront is 'as cold and heavy as a rock of ice.' Woman is termed 'falsest fair' as in *Weathercock.* Both the Queen and Lady Bright desire the society of their lovers but are afraid to entrust themselves to it. To Euphanes the Queen says:

> . . . . troth have I wished
> A thousand times that I had been a man,
> That I might sit a day with thee alone,
> And talk.
>
> Act III. 1, p. 442.

Lady Bright can hardly bear to dismiss Bold and confesses:

> . . . I swear by Heaven,
> I would spend all night to sit and talk w'ye,
> If I durst trust you.
>
> *Amends,* Act IV. 1, p. 464.

Perhaps the most interesting resemblance is that between the ravings of Onos in love and of the rejected Sir Abraham Ninny:

> Oh,
> Black clouds of discontent invelope me!
> Garters, fly off; go hatband, bind the brows
> Of some dull citizen that fears to ache:
> And, leg, appear now in simplicity,
> Without the trappings of a courtier;
> Burst, buttons, burst, your Bachelor is worm'd!
> . . . .
> Burn, eyes, out in your sockets, sink and stink.
>
> *Queen of Corinth,* Act IV. 1, p. 455.

Well since I am disdained, off garters blue!
Which signify Sir Abram's love was true;
Off, cypress black! for thou befits not me;
Thou art not cypress of the cypress tree, ˙
Befitting lovers. Out, green shoestrings, out!
Wither in pocket, since my Luce doth pout.
Gush, eyes; thump, hand; swell, heart: buttons, fly open!
Thanks, gentle doublet, else my heart had broken.

Weathercock, Act I. 2, p. 359.

The power of virtue is also similarly expressed by Euphanes
and by Seldom in *Amends:*

Mischief, 'gainst goodness aim'd is like a stone,
Unnaturally forc'd up an eminent hill,
Whose weight falls on our heads and buries us;
We springe ourselves, we sink in our own bogs.

Queen of Corinth, Act IV. 4, p. 467.

Virtue's a solid rock, whereat being aim'd
The keenest darts of envy, yet unhurt
Her marble heroes stand, built of such bases,
Whilst they recoil, and wound the shooter's faces.

Queen of Corinth, Act III. 1, p. 443.

. . . even as dirt thrown hard against a wall,
Rebounds and sparkles in the thrower's eyes,
So ill words, uttered to a virtuous dame
Turn and defile the speaker with red shame.

Amends, Act II. 1, p. 438.

There are a number of parallels between these acts of the
Queen of Corinth, the *Fatal Dowry,* and the first two
Triumphs. The pine and oak figure is used to picture the
relationship between the Queen and Euphanes in *Queen of
Corinth* and between Romont and the deceased marshal in the
Fatal Dowry. Of Euphanes it is said:

. . . . . like a young pine
He grows up planted under a fair oak.

Queen of Corinth, Act III. 1, p. 436.

Charalois says Romont like:

> A hearty oak, grew'st close to this tall pine.
>
> *The Fatal Dowry*, Act II. 1, p. 113.

Rochfort, however, thinks of Charalois himself as:

> A goodly oak whereon to twist my vine.
>
> *The Fatal Dowry*, Act II. 2, p. 120.

The figure of the divided stream occurs in both plays:

> Nature's divided streams the highest shelf
> Will over-run at last, and flow to itself.
>
> *Queen of Corinth*, Act IV. 4, p. 471.

> Like crystal tears rivers individually
> Flow into one another, make one source.
>
> *The Fatal Dowry*, Act II. 2, p. 126.

One also finds repeated from the *Induction* to the *Four Plays,* the idea that the grateful person is a tributary stream:

> I came to tender you the man you have made,
> And, like a thankful stream, to retribute
> All you, my ocean, have enrich'd me with.
>
> *Queen of Corinth*, Act III. 2, p. 451.

> Majestic ocean, that with plenty feeds
> Me, thy poor tributary rivulet;
> ....
> Curs'd be my birth-hour, and my ending day,
> When back your love-floods I forget to pay!
>
> *Induction*, p. 482.

Storms play their part in helping us to realize just how the characters are moved:

> She chafes like storms in groves, now sighs, now weeps,
> And both sometimes, like rain and wind commix'd.
>
> *Queen of Corinth*, Act IV. 3, p. 466.

> I weep sometimes, and instantly can laugh:
> Nay, I do dance, and sing, and suddenly
> Roar like a storm.
>
> *Triumph of Love*, Scene III, p. 522.

The scales figure, also, had been previously used in the
Triumph of Love:

> When in the scales
> Nature and fond affection weigh together,
> One poises like a feather.
>
> *Queen of Corinth,* Act IV. 3, p. 463.

> Thy person and thy virtues, in one scale,
> Shall poise hers with her beauty and her wealth.
>
> *Triumph of Love,* Scene II, p. 514.

The book figure in which life is called a fair book and an
evil deed, the black page is found in the *Queen of Corinth,*
the *Triumph of Honour,* and the *Knight of Malta:*

> . . . . when posterity
> Shall read your volumes fill'd with virtuous acts,
> And shall arrive at this black bloody leaf,
> Noting your foolish barbarism, and my wrong,
> (As time shall make it plain,) what follows this,
> Decyphering any noble deed of yours,
> Shall be quite lost, for men will read no more.
>
> *Queen of Corinth,* Act IV. 3, p. 464.

> When men shall read the records of thy valour,
> Thy hitherto-brave virtue, and approach
> (Highly content yet) to this foul assault
> Included in this leaf, this ominous leaf,
> They shall throw down the book, and read no more.
>
> *Triumph of Honour,* Scene II, p. 499.

> Think on the legend which we two shall breed,
> Continuing as we are, for chastest dames
> And boldest soldiers to peruse and read,
> Ay, and read thorough, free from any act
> To cause the modest cast the book away,
> And the most honour'd captain fold it up.
>
> *Knight of Malta,* Act V. 1, p. 194.

Though no one of the above tests for authorship applied
to Acts III and IV of the *Queen of Corinth* is alone conclusive proof of Field's hand, the cumulative evidence signi-
fies that the writing is his.

The *Knight of Malta* has gone through many stages in the assignation of authorship. Dyce gives it to Fletcher àlone. Macaulay (*Francis Beaumont*, p. 196) gives Act V to Beaumont, but later (*C. H. L.* VI, p. 156) he divides it: Fletcher, Acts II, III. 1, and IV. 2, 3, 4; Massinger, Acts III. 2 and IV. 1 (?); and third author, Acts I and V. He says, 'The style of the third author is somewhat like that of Field, but better than his usual work.' Fleay (*E. S.* XIII, p. 34 and *Drama* I, pp. 205-6) gives it to Fletcher, Massinger and Field, dividing it thus: Fletcher, Acts II, III. 1, 4, and IV. 2, 3, 4; Massinger, Acts III. 2, 3, and IV. 1; and Field, Acts I and V. Boyle (*E. S.* V, p. 75) found 'besides Beaumont and Fletcher, a third hand;' in *Englische Studien* VIII, pp. 46-50, he gives proof that Massinger is the third author detected in Act III. 1, 2. He does not change his earlier statement that Beaumont wrote Acts I and V, and Fletcher, Acts II, III. 1, 4, and IV. 2, 3, 4. Oliphant (*E. S.* XVI, pp. 181-4) suggests that 'it is probable that this play is a revision by Fletcher, Massinger, and Field of an old (unacted) play of Beaumont's.' He divides it: Fletcher, Acts II. 1, III. 1, 4, IV. 2, 4b; Field, Acts I and V; Massinger, Acts III. 2, 3, and IV. 1, 3-4a.[19] Bullen (*D. N. B.*) assigns Acts II and III. 1 to Fletcher; Acts III. 2, 3, IV. 1, and V. 2 to Massinger; and Act I and part of Act V to 'some other.' Gayley (*Beaumont, the Dramatist*, p. 378) says that there is no satisfactory evidence of Beaumont. Sykes (*S. E. D.*, pp. 214-7) attributes Acts I and V to Field. Chambers (*E. Stage* III, p. 218) does not discuss authorship.

From the list of actors the play must be dated 1618 or the beginning of 1619;[20] Beaumont, therefore, could have

[19] This division is repeated 'practically unchanged' by Oliphant in 1927 (*op. cit.*, p. 394), but Field is credited with Acts I and V 'very hesitatingly,' p. 395.
[20] Oliphant (*op. cit.*, pp. 392-3) dates both this play and the *Queen of Corinth* 1616. If my evidence for the date of Field's joining the King's Men be correct, the plays must be later than 1616.

no hand in the play. The application of a number of tests to Acts I and V identify them as the work of Field. Boyle's tables for this play (*E. S.* V) yield 13.7% double endings and 21% run-on lines for Act I, and 19.5% double endings and 25% run-on lines for Act V. In this play Massinger averages about 49% double endings and 31% run-on lines; and Fletcher, 66% double endings and 9% run-on lines, so that the line of demarcation is unmistakable. The preponderance of final important pauses over medial important pauses also aids in showing Field. In Act I there are 177 final important pauses and 115 medial important pauses; in Act V there are 165 final important pauses and 93 medial important pauses.

It is Scene I of Act V, the scene in which Oriana's eloquent pleading converts Miranda's passion to spiritual love, that some critics have felt to be too moral for Field. Sir A. W. Ward thinks that there is 'no nobler vindication of the authority of the moral in the whole range of the Elizabethan Drama.'[21] It has also been highly praised in *Le Théatre Français et Anglais:* 'La tragédie "The Knight of Malta" contient une scène,—le Ve du Ier acte: conseils d'Oriana à Miranda,—qui, par l'élévation des sentiments, est peut-être la plus belle du Drame Elizabéthéen.'[22] The authorship is attributed to Beaumont.

I feel that there is sufficient evidence to assign the scene to Field, though, doubtless, it is his best piece of writing. The situation is one on which twice previously he had tried his hand. In Act IV. 1 of *Amends* Lady Bright argues with Bold against physical passion. It is true that she reinforces her argument with a sword and with threats of crying out, yet her pleading is along the same line as that of Oriana:

---

[21] *History of English Dramatic Literature* 2. 688.
[22] Charles Hastings, *Le Théatre Français et Anglais* (Paris, 1900), p. 326.

> . . . . Upon my knees
> I do desire thee to preserve thy virtues,
> And with my tears my honour: 'tis as bad
> To lose our worths to them, or to deceive
> Who have held worthy opinions of us,
> As to betray trust, All this I implore
> For thine own sake, not mine.
> ....
> . . . . I had rather far confound
> The dearest body in the world to me,
> Than that body should confound my soul.
>
> *Amends,* Act IV. 1, p. 463.

She even threatens to fall upon the sword herself, if there is no other way to save her honor. Having persuaded Bold to follow reason, the one quality that makes man 'the prince of creatures,' she admits her love; nevertheless, she resolutely drives Bold forth. Bold changes his opinion of woman and admits to his friend, Welltried, that he was 'such an erroneous heretic to love and women as thou art, till now.' In Scenes II and IV of *Triumph of Honour* Dorigen argues with Martius, recalling the fine record of his past life:

> Oh, Martius, Martius, wouldst thou in one minute
> Blast all thy laurels, which so many years
> Thou hast been purchasing with blood and sweat?
>
> Scene II, p. 499.

Then, like Oriana, she uses the book figure and points out how this one 'foul assault' will ruin the whole story.[23] Unable to change Martius by pleading, she offers to stab herself. This convinces Martius of her purity. Kneeling, he seeks forgiveness and questions, 'Was ever such a woman?'

Miranda's attitude toward Oriana is that characteristic of Field's men. 'I have touch'd thee' says Miranda in an aside:

[23] Cf. parallel passages.

> Hold but this test, so rich an ore was never
> Tried by the hand of man on the vast earth.
>
>   Act V. 1, p. 193.

Miranda is astonished that Oriana can resist his overtures
and with growing wonder exclaims:

> Find such another woman
> And take her for his labor any man!
>
>   Act V. 1, p. 194.

When he restores Oriana to Gomera, it is with these words:

> . . . . busy Nature,
> If thou wilt still make women, but remember
> To work 'em by this sampler.
>
>   Act V. 2, p. 202.

At first Oriana's arguments have the same effect upon
Miranda that Dorigen's do upon Martius. The fineness
of the argument is admitted, but it stirs passion to even
greater heights. In all three plays it is the remarkable
inflexibility of the women that finally convinces the men
that here at last is one woman who is not as 'insatiate as the
grave.' Oriana is not, I think, a Beaumont creation. The
very fact that she has to protest her chastity marks her as
different from Beaumont's women. She is stirred by
Miranda's presence and admits, 'My flames, Miranda, rise
as high as thine.' Like Lady Bright in *Amends,* she really
wishes to give in, but, as a matter of principle, she will not
allow herself to do so.

Another repeated situation is that of the discovery scene
in Act V. 2. Oriana, who is thought to be dead, comes in
veiled. When she unveils, there are various exclamations.
After this excitement loses edge, Colonna throws off his
disguise, and Lucinda screams, 'My husband, my dearest
Angelo.' One recalls the scene in *Triumph of Love* where
Cornelia unveils and is recognized by Rinaldo as his wife,
and the discovery scenes in Field's individual plays.

It has been noted that Field, like Jonson, refers to the beauty mask. Zanthia mentions the nightly 'blanching water' and 'smoothing oils,' but does not give the ingredients as did Bold in *Annals* (Act III. 3, p. 454). Zanthia, however, adds other interesting details in regard to the seventeenth century woman's efforts to beautify herself (Act I. 1, pp. 112-3).

In both Acts I and V the characterization is like that of Field. The women especially seem drawn by Field's hand. As has been shown, Oriana is closely related to Lady Bright in *Amends*. Zanthia, in contrast with Oriana, is all body. She is outspoken concerning her desires and gives herself up in abandonment to her passionate emotion. Incidentally, the very fact that her name is changed from Abdella to Zanthia denotes a change of author. In Act I. 2 two gentlewomen, who never become personalities, are introduced for the sole purpose of discussing marriage in the indelicate manner of Field's women. The male characters have a very light opinion of women. Even Valetta, who, it seems, should know the fine character of his sister, immediately believes Mountferrat's accusation that she is a traitor and silences her with:

> Peace, thou fair sweet bank of flowers,
> Under whose beauty Scorpions lie and kill.
>
> Act I. 3, p. 123.

Women cannot please Mountferrat, for he believes:

> . . . . . . Woman then
> Checking or granting is the grave of men.
>
> Act I. 1, p. 111.

In fact, woman disturbs him so much that he is driven to implore:

> Pish—woman—memory,
> Would one of ye would leave me.
>
> Act I. 1, p. 111.

The lines are full of that Fieldian vehemence which indicates imitation of Beaumont. Mountferrat's first speech is given in the unmistakable, windy rhetoric of Field:

> Tempests I have subdu'd, and fought 'em calm,
> Out-lighten'd lightening in my chivalry,
> Rid tame as patience billows that kick'd heaven,
> Whistled enragèd Boreas till his gusts
> Were grown so gentle that he seem'd to sigh
> Because he could not show the air my keel.
>
> Act I. 1, p. 107.

Gomera declares:

> I
> Will cram this slander back into thy throat,
> And with my sword's point thrust it to thy heart,
> . . . .
> I will tear those spurs
> Off from thy heels and stick 'em in thy front,
> As a mark'd villain.
>
> Act I. 3, p. 124.

Again with Field-like abandon he exclaims:

> All breath I'll spend in sighs, all sound in groans,
> And know no company but my wasting moans.
>
> Act V. 2, p. 197.

The two songs in Act V. 2 are also indications of Field's writing. Opposite themes are used in the songs as in those in the *Queen of Corinth*.

Though the style is better than that of Field's early work, explanatory material is still dragged into the lines in the crude way shown in the following examples:

> . . . . With reverence
> To our Great-master and this consistory,
> (I have consider'd it, it cannot be)
> Thou art a villain.
>
> Act I. 3, p. 124.

> I must deliver in
> (The year expir'd) my probation weed.
>
> Act V. 1, p. 192.

The figurative language is that found recurring in Field's work. Love is a 'violent flood;' Mountferrat feels a 'torrent of joy;' a pearl can turn 'strong streams' sooner than Mountferrat can move Oriana. The lives of Oriana and Miranda make a book, and Miranda's story is to be fixed in heaven. Nature makes people by her patterns. If she insists upon making women, Miranda wants her to use Oriana as the pattern. Gomera, however, doubts Nature's ability to make such another. The jewel figure becomes specific, for we are told that Zanthia is a pearl. That we may picture her more perfectly, we are informed that she is as straight as young pines and cedars in a grove. In spite of her attractions she fears that she will be like a stage property discarded. The mathematical figure is used in connection with the relation between husbands and wives: the second gentlewoman does not want a husband that 'sails by his wife's compass;' wives are compared to 'superficial lines in geometry.' It is Lucinda's body that is a case this time—a 'beauteous case' for her Turkish soul. As is usual with Field, certain characters are seen as animals: Zanthia is a 'black swan,' a 'branded bitch,' and a 'Barbary mare;' Mountferrat is a 'damned hell-hound' and a 'French stallion.' Many classical allusions are brought in to give point to the comparisons: Boreas, Zephyrus, Cupid, Ixion, Juno, Europa, Phlegethon, and Cocytus.

The stage technique is that of Field. The opening line, 'Dares she despise me thus?' at once arouses interest and plunges us into the story. This question affords an excellent device for Mountferrat's telling us of his great deeds which make him merit Oriana's favor, and for the ensuing explanatory dialogue between Mountferrat and Rocco. The story moves forward rapidly, and the lines are used for narrative and action rather than for characterization or poetic adornment. One interesting bit of technique shows, I think, that the author of Act I was again taking up the story in Act V. Gomera is made to summarize the story as a background for the solution that immediately follows, (Act V. 2, pp. 197-8). The dialogue is frequently given force by the fact that all the characters speak out in concert. This device is used five times in Act V and an equal number of times in one scene in Act I (scene 3). The entrances and exits are prepared with extreme care. Sometimes the entering character is identified by one already on the stage as when Mountferrat gives both Rocco's name and position by greeting him, 'Rocco, my trusty servant.' In Act V. 2 the characters are announced. Miranda clears the stage for his dialogue with Oriana by giving Colonna a job and asking Lucinda to depart. Stage directions are found even where the lines make the accompanying action unmistákable. For example, Mountferrat says, 'Is this your hand?' and the direction follows, 'Showing a letter;' Gomera says, 'Take, if thou dar'st, that gage,' and the direction reads, 'Throws down his glove.' The stage directions are also very full and explicit. When Mountferrat is to be withdrawn from the order, we find this direction: 'Music. A curtain is drawn. An altar discovered, with tapers and a book on it. Two Bishops stand on each side of it. Mountferrat, as the song is singing, is led up to the altar.' The maximum of stage effectiveness is thrown into these two acts. The processions (at the beginning of Acts I. 3 and V. 2) are fine pieces of pageantry. The falling of Montferrat's cross, the sensational revelation of Oriana's letter to the basha of Tripoli just as Oriana with her ladies descended from the gallery to be betrothed to Gomera, Gomera's and Mountferrat's flying gages, the discovery that Miranda's veiled captive is Oriana, Colonna's revelation that he is Angelo, the degrading in Mountferrat and the investiture of Miranda— all are excellent stage business.

The vocabulary of these acts is surely Field's. *Innocent* is used four times; *innocence*, twice; *continence*, three times; *chastity*, six times; *chaste*, four times; *beauteous*, *pish*, and *humph* are also found recurring. *Conventing*, in the sense of being gathered together, is used here as in

Weathercock. Other expressions that sound like Field are: *gentlier, fitlier, 'fraughted home, explicate your thoughts,* to *oppugne the Christian enemy,* and to *indue a robe. Neglects, helps,* and *remove* are used as nouns. In both acts the use of *'gainst, 'fore, 'cause,* and *'bout* as well as *'scaping* seems to denote the hand of Field. *Ye* occurs as object as well as subject, and there is an occasional careless shift in the use of pronouns, such as in the line, 'I'll knock *you* thus together, wear *ye* out' (Act I. 3, p. 126). There are only six of Beaumont's words and phrases appearing in the two acts and these are unrepeated—*beast, bull, fate, ages consequent, load of grief,* and *infectious.* Of these the first three are not used in Beaumont's usual manner.

Sykes has pointed out the striking resemblance between Dorigen's appeal to the honor of Martius and Oriana's appeal to the purity of Miranda. He parallels the sections thus:[24]

> Oh, Martius, Martius! wouldst thou in one minute
> Blast all thy laurels, which so many years
> Thou hast been purchasing with blood and sweat?
> Hath Dorigen never been written, read,
> Without the epithet of chaste, chaste Dorigen,
> And wouldst thou fall upon her chastity,
> Like a black drop of ink, to blot it out?
> > *Triumph of Honour,* Scene II, p. 499.

> . . . . . . Miranda's deeds
> Have been as white as Oriana's fame,
> From the beginning to this point of time,
> And shall we now begin to stain both thus?
> > *Knight of Malta,* Act IV. 1, p. 194.

Dorigen, continued:

> When men shall read the records of thy valour,
> Thy hitherto-brave virtue, and approach
> (Highly content yet) to this foul assault
> Included in this leaf, this ominous leaf,
> They shall throw down the book, and read no more.

[24] Sykes, *op. cit.,* p. 215.

Oriana, continued:

> Think on the legend which we two shall breed,
> Continuing as we are, for chastest dames
> And boldest soldiers to peruse and read,
> Ay, and read thorough, free from any act
> To cause the modest cast the book away,
> And the most honour'd captain fold it up.

Martius:

> Oh, thou confut'st divinely, and thy words
> Do fall like rods upon me! but they have
> Such silken lines and silver hooks, that I
> Am faster snar'd.

Miranda:

> Oh, what a tongue is here! whilst she doth teach
> My heart to hate my fond unlawful love,
> She talks me more in love, with love to her;
> My fire she quenched with her arguments,
> But as she breathes 'em they blow fresher fires.

There are also passages which closely parallel passages in *Amends:*

> . . . . . thy pleas'd eyes send forth
> Beams brighter than the star that ushers day.
>
> > *Knight of Malta,* Act I. 1, p. 108.

> All want day, till thy beauty rise
> For the grey morn breaks from thine eyes.
>
> > *Amends,* Act IV. 1, p. 465.

Compare *The Fatal Dowry,* Act II. 2, p. 119:

> . . . . . . a fairer sun doth rise
> From the bright radiance of my mistress' eyes.

Oriana speaks of herself as one:

> That has been sold, us'd, and lost her show!
> I am a garment worn.
>
> > *Knight of Malta,* Act V. 1, 195.

> *Lady Perfect.* A wife is like a garment us'd and torn.
> *Lady Bright.* A widow is a garment worn threadbare
> Selling at second-hand, like broker's ware.
>
> > *Amends,* Act I. 1, p. 419.

The authorship of *Honest Man's Fortune* has been much discussed. Dyce gives the play to Beaumont and Fletcher. Fleay (*Drama* I, p. 196) thinks it the play of 'Mr. Fletcher and ours' mentioned in the letter to Henslowe about 1613 and signed by Field, Massinger, and Daborne.[25] He assigns to Field Acts III. 1, 2, 3, and IV. 1, 2; to Massinger, Acts I and II. 1; to Daborne, Act II. 2-4; and to Fletcher, Act V. Boyle changes from his first division of the play (*E. S.* V, pp. 75-9) in which he gives Acts I-II. 1 to a third, Acts II. 2-IV. 2 to Beaumont, and Act V to Fletcher. Later (*E. S.* VIII, pp. 40-6) he divides the play: Tourneur, Act I and Act II. 1; Massinger, Act III; Beaumont, Act IV; and Fletcher, Act V. Oliphant (*E. S.* XV, pp. 327-31) makes a complicated division,[26] ascribing to Field a large part of Act II, a part of Act III. 3, and Act IV. 1, 2b. Bullen (*D. N. B.*) thinks that Field's authorship of Act IV and a part of Act III is 'very plausible.' Macaulay (*C. H. L.* VI, p. 156) finds four authors: Tourneur, Act I; Massinger, Act III. 1; Field, Act IV; Fletcher, Act V; the 'rest doubtful.' Gayley (*Beaumont, the Dramatist*, p. 378) does not find Beaumont in the play. Sykes (*S. E. D.*, pp. 217-8) says, 'Field may have been concerned in Act IV,' but finds 'nothing whatever to suggest Field in Act III' and points out the possibility of Webster's authorship. Chambers (*E. Stage* III, p. 227) agrees that Massinger is in Act III and that Fletcher wrote Act V, but terms the attribution of the remainder of the play 'a quagmire of conjecture.'

Although there are a few passages not unlike Field in Act II. 2b-5, I do not see sufficient evidence for assigning the

---

[25] Greg, *Henslowe Papers*, p. 65.

[26] *Field*, II. 2b-5, III. 3b, IV. 1, 2b; *Unknown*, I. 1-3. II. 1(?). 2a (to Dubois' entry); *Fletcher*, V. 1-3; *Massinger*, III. 1-3a (to Mal.'s exit); *Massinger* and *Field*, IV. 2a (to Lam.'s entry). In *The Plays of Beaumont and Fletcher*, pp. 384-5, he adds Tourneur and Webster to the list of collaborators and assigns to Field II. 4b, IV, V. 3b.

work to him.   The prose moves too heavily, and the verse lacks Field's buoyancy.   Metrical tests for Act III do not indicate Field, and Boyle has, I think, made a good case for Massinger's authorship.

Act IV is the only part of the play which shows decisive evidence of being wholly by Field.   The metrical tests very strongly indicate his authorship: 17% double endings and 18% run-on lines are normal figures for Field and present a noticeable contrast to the higher figures for the remainder of the play.   Here, too, there are 224 final important pauses and only 108 medial important pauses.

The duel scene is handled in much the same manner as in *Amends* and *Queen of Corinth*.   When the duelists are ready, their attendants are dismissed just as Frank and Lady Honour in *Amends* are asked to walk away.   Just as the first blows fall, the lady in the case rushes in and ends the combat.   Orleans begs, 'Give me one stroke yet at thee for my vengeance' (Act IV. 2, p. 423), recalling Crates's petition for 'one stroke for fear of laughter' (*Queen of Corinth,* Act IV. 4, p. 468).

The sycophants and the page are Fieldian characters. Veramour could not, I think, be Beaumont's.   Though sentimental, he is not more sentimental than Lady Honour when she is a page.   It is interesting to note that both refer to the especial duty of running by the horse's side.   Veramour is far more pert than Beaumont's page characters and is almost unpardonable in the scene with Charlotte (Act IV. 1, pp. 413-4).   One cannot imagine one of Beaumont's charming pages as saying, 'Never stir, but you are the troublesomest ass that e'er I met with' (Act IV. 1, p. 419). Because Veramour is really a boy, he can indulge in a type of playful naughtiness wholly foreign to an Urania.   He, like other Field characters, has a low opinion of woman. He tells Montague, 'I had rather trust you by a roaring lion than a ravening woman' (Act IV. 1, p. 412).   He feels, too, that Montague's mind is stronger than to 'credit woman's vows, and too sure to be capable of their loves' (Act IV. 1, p. 413). The women are independent in spirit, and instead of submitting to misfortune, they go about righting it. Lamira wants Montague; she takes him into her service and gets Charlotte to woo him for her. The Duchess orders a caroch and drives furiously to the dueling grounds to stop the duel between her husband and her brother. The leading characters give excellent descriptive sketches of each other, but they do not let us get acquainted with them at first hand. They are presented from an outside point of view instead of being developed from within.

There are several references to contemporary life. Veramour speaks of the 'worldly qualities' which some of 'our scarlet gallants teach their boys.' La-Poop alludes to the long staves of the watermen. Laverdine mentions the fact that the beautiful wife of the tradesman will draw custom to his shop. Seldom in *Amends* thought it was remarkable that his wife could remain in the shop and stay honest. Mention of law is made in the usual satirical manner. Montague knows that the Duke's greatness 'may corrupt a jury and make a judge afraid.'

There is some rhetoric in this act, which could scarcely have been written by anyone except Field. Longueville explains:

> My reverence is unto this man, my master,
> Whom you, with protestations and oaths
> As high as Heaven, as deep as Hell, which would
> Deceive the wisest man of honest nature,
> Have cozen'd and abus'd.
>
> Act IV. 1, p. 418.

Orleans will fight anywhere:

> Upon a bridge, a rail but my sword's breadth,
> Upon a battlement, I'll fight this quarrel.
>
> Act IV. 2, p. 420.

Amiens declares to Orleans:

> Thou shalt have strokes and strokes, thou glorious man,
> Till thou breath'st thinner air than that thou talk'st.
>
> Act IV. 2, p. 423.

In the general quarrel scene, Lamira rebukes Amiens:

> Stand'st thou looking upon the mischief thou hast made?
> Thou godless man, feeding thy blood-shot eyes
> With the red spectacle, and art not turn'd to stone
> With horror? Hence, and take the wings of the black
> Infamy, to carry thee beyond the shoot of looks,
> Or sound of curses, which will pursue thee still:
> Thou hast out-fled all but thy guilt.
>
> Act IV. 2, p. 427.

Orleans threatens to grow:

> Unto this earth, 'till I have wept a trench
> That shall be great enough to be my grave.
>
> Act IV. 2, p. 428.

It is a wit like Field's that prompts the quick reply to Charlotte's question:

> *Char.* Are you in post, sir?
> *Long.* No, I am in satin, lady.
>
> Act IV. 1, p. 416.

The change of name from Anabella to Lamira in this act indicates a change of author and recalls the fact that Field changed the name of a character in his part of the *Knight of Malta.*

Explanation which seems necessary for the purpose of clearness is dragged into the dialogue regardless of the appropriateness of its place. Montague explains to Veramour:

> . . . . . But my desire
> Is, thou wouldst not (as thou usest still,
> When, like a servant, I 'mong servants sit)
> Wait on my trencher.
>
> Act IV. 1, p. 411.

Veramour offers his master some money, but since it is not clear where Veramour could have got money, he puts the explanation into his plea for acceptance. To prepare for the scene between Laverdine and Veramour, Mallicorn makes a totally irrelevant remark in the midst of engrossing action (Act IV. 1, p. 418).

In the figurative language the idea recurs that the body is a repository for the spirit. Veramour is a 'beauteous cabinet to lock up all the goodness of the earth.' Nature made him thus, but whether in a frame or by a pattern is not mentioned! Charlotte is 'Nature's heir' in feature. The book figure is found in this act when Veramour speaks of Montague's misfortune and his own loyalty as making a story 'to make every hearer weep.' The interruption of the duel is called an interlude and the interruptors, actors.

The handling of the stagecraft aids in discerning Field. One is never left in doubt as to who is coming upon the scene or what the relationship between the characters is. Montague enters, uttering his own name; Veramour sees Charlotte and exclaims, 'I have lost my voice with the very sight of this gentlewoman;' and so on. The scenes are managed for the effect from the point of view of the audience. When Charlotte kneels to Montague, down goes Montague on his knees, also. In the duel scene pistols are used as well as swords. In the violent railing scene which follows the interruption of the duel, Longueville shoots, and Lady Orleans falls, apparently dead. Orleans falls in grief. The audience has already had its thrill before Longueville reveals that the pistol was charged with powder only, and that the lady is merely in a faint from fright.

The vocabulary of this act seems to bear the mark of Field. There are *innocent* and *innocence, gyves, plenteous, beauteous, forfeit* and the customary line of exclamations and oaths. *Scoff* and *hates* are used as nouns, and *plainlier* for the adverbial form; *manacle* is used as a verb, a construction also found in *Triumph of Honour*. The forms, *'mong, 'gainst, 'twixt,* and *'ware,* also designate Field. *'Em* is used for *them;* occurring three times as often as the latter. Phrases found in Field's other work are recurrent here. Of Montague it is said that misfortune is a 'poor cloud, eclipseth all thy splendor.' Charlotte considers him 'the very sun of France,' but Montague replies, 'I am in the eclipse now;' Martius in *Triumph of Honour* is also said to be in eclipse and is to rise like the sun. The Duke of Orleans cries out, 'Art thou there, basilisk?' just as Dorigen did when she saw Martius; Bellafront, in *Weathercock,* would have the basilisk gone, 'O basilisk, remove thee from my sight.' Life as material for a story is an idea repeated in *Four Plays, Queen of Corinth,* and *Knight of Malta.*

The closest parallel is between the lines of Veramour and Oriana. Veramour tells Montague:

> . . . . . thus we'll breed a story
> To make every hearer weep.
>
> Act IV. 1, p. 411.

Oriana reminds Miranda that their conduct is not a matter of the moment only:

> Think of the legend which we two shall breed.
>
> *Knight of Malta,* Act V. 1, p. 194.

The very fact that only one of a number of critics working on the same body of plays gives work by an unknown hand to Field is, in itself, evidence of the vagueness of the attribution. Fleay is the only critic who sees Field in *The Laws of Candy* (*E. S.* IX, p. 23) and in *Thierry and Theodoret* (*E. S.* XIII, p. 34). In only one of four publications does Fleay assign any part of *The Laws of Candy* to Field. In 1874 (*T. S. S.* I, p. 60) he says, 'I cannot trace the authors of this play, but there are two.' He points out Acts II. 1 and III. 3 as different from the remainder of the play. In 1886 (*E. S.* IX, p. 23) he suggests that the play is the work of Massinger and Field with a small share by Fletcher, but he makes no attempt to divide the play. In his paper on Field (*E. S.* XIII, pp. 28ff.) he does not mention this play. In his final writing on the subject (*Drama* I, p. 209) he attributes the play wholly to Massinger and sees revision by Fletcher. Boyle first gave the play to Shirley (*E. S.* VII, p. 75) but later withdrew the suggestion since Shirley did not come to London before 1624 (*E. S.* XVIII, p. 294). Oliphant (*E. S.* XV, pp. 333-5) believes the play written about 1604-5 by Beaumont and Fletcher and revised for the stage by Massinger about 1620.[27] Bullen (*D. N. B.*) thinks it belongs largely to Massinger, but also detects Fletcher. Gayley (*Beaumont, the Dramatist,* p. 378) and Chambers (*E. Stage* III, p. 218) merely exclude the play from Beaumont's work. Sykes (*S. E. D.,* p. 224) lists Acts I, IV. 2, and V as Massinger; Act III. 1, 2 as a second author; and Acts II, III. 3, and IV. 1 as collaborative. The second author, he says, is not Beaumont or Field.

The actor list of the play contains the name of neither Burbadge nor Field, but does give Joseph Taylor. It would seem, therefore, that the play must belong to a date following Burbadge's death, for Taylor's name is not found among the King's Men until March 19 of that year (Hist. MSS. IV, p. 299). Taylor was a member of Prince Charles's Company in January when Middleton's *Mask of Heroes* was performed. Probably he joined the King's Men after Burbadge's death. Since Field was gone from the stage before the production of *Barnavelt* in August, and the name of his successor, John Rice, appears on the actor list, it seems very probable that the play is too late for Field to have been concerned with it. Certainly neither style nor handling of plot is like Field. I think that we may safely assume that he had nothing to do with the play. Metrical tests support this conclusion, for Act III. 1 has 38% double endings and 28% run-on lines and Act III. 2 has 37% double endings and 40% run-on lines.

[27] In *The Plays of Beaumont and Fletcher,* p. 481, he attributes the play to Ford with 'one little bit of Fletcher.'

Dyce finds only Beaumont and Fletcher in *Thierry and Theodoret*. Fleay (*T. S. S.* (1874), p. 64) divides the play between Beaumont and Fletcher. Later (*E. S.* XIII, p. 34) he divides it between Fletcher (I. 1, II. 2, 3, IV. 1, V. 2), Massinger (I. 2, II. 1, IV. 2), and Field (II. 4, III. 1, 2, and V. 1). Boyle (*E. S.* V, p. 93, VIII, pp. 57-61 and IX, p. 21) is unable to recognize the third hand which he detects in Acts III and V. 1. Oliphant (*E. S.* XV, pp. 352-3) says that the play was written about 1607-8 by Fletcher and Beaumont, or by Beaumont alone, and was revised in 1617 by Massinger, or by Massinger and Field.[28] He makes the following division:

> Massinger, I. 2, II. 1, 4a (to Thierry's exit), III. 2a, IV. 2.
> Fletcher, I. 1b, II. 2-3, IV. 1, V. 2.
> Beaumont, III. 2b (from Thierry's entry).
> Massinger and Fletcher, I. 1a (first 4 speeches).
> Massinger and Beaumont, II. 4b (?), III. 1, V. 1a.
> Fletcher and Beaumont, V. 1b.

Bullen (*D. N. B.*) says 'no portion of *Thierry and Theodoret* can be confidently given to Beaumont.' He divides it between Massinger, Fletcher, and a third to whom he assigns Act III. Macaulay, who had followed Fleay's division in 1883 (*Francis Beaumont* (London, 1883), p. 94) with the exception that he gave to Beaumont the work Fleay attributed to Field, is unable to identify the author of Acts III and V. 1, in 1910 (*C. H. L.* VI, p. 156). Gayley (*Beaumont, the Dramatist*, pp. 387-8) says the play 'is a later production by Fletcher, Massinger, and one other.' Sykes (*S. E. D.*, p. 218) does not find any suggestion of Field. Chambers (*E. Stage* III, p. 218) merely lists it as of doubtful authorship.

Oliphant points out one difficulty that cannot be explained if Fleay's theory of authorship is accepted; this is Massinger's alteration of Field's original writing in Acts II. 4,

---

[28] In his new study the alterations are 'very slight' (*op. cit.*, p. 278).

III. 1, and V. 1. He is able to show Massinger's presence in these scenes by 353 examples. By metrical tests Act III is the only portion of the play that could possibly be Field's. I can see no indication of Field except the use of rhyme and the single occurrence of a few words used by Field, but not restricted to his vocabulary. The prose of these scenes is totally unlike Field's. One familiar with the vigor and rapid play of Field's prose would find it impossible to conceive of his being the author of lines written with so much repetition and hesitation as the following:

> Gentlemen, as you are gentlemen, spare my letters, and take all, willingly all: I'll give you a release, a general release, and meet you here tomorrow with as much more.
>
> * * * * * *
>
> Would we were all lost, hang'd, quarter'd, to save this one, one innocent Prince; Thierry's poison'd, by his mother poison'd, the Mistress to this stallion, who by that poison ne'er shall sleep again.

Fleay and Macaulay both think that Field had a hand in *Bonduca.* Fleay (*Drama* I, p. 203) points out a second writer and suggests that he may be Field. Macaulay (*C. H. L.* VI, p. 156), with some hesitation, indicates Acts II. 1 and IV as Field's share. With the exception of Oliphant (*E. S.* XV, p. 335), who thinks the play an early work of Beaumont's revised by Fletcher,[29] other critics assign this play to Fletcher alone. External evidence would prevent the assignation of any part of this play to Field. It is a King's Men play produced before 1614, for Ostler's name appears on the actor list and Ostler died in 1614. As Field was not connected with the King's Men until some three years later, any allotment of a share in this play to him would be extremely hazardous. An examination of the style and vocabulary of the two brief scenes assigned to Field does not

---

[29] Oliphant now suggests that the play is early Fletcher (*op. cit.,* pp. 133-4).

reveal any evidence of his presence. Metrical tests also show that Field did not write these scenes, for in all of Field's known work the percentage of double endings is lower than that of run-on lines, and these scenes reverse the order. Act II. 1 has 31.6% double endings and 11.7% run-on lines, and Act IV. 4 has 40% double endings and 13.5% run-on lines.

The critics agree that there are three or four collaborators concerned with the *Bloody Brother,* and several see Field. Dyce, however, gives it to Fletcher and Rowley. Fleay in 1874 (*T. S. S.,* p. 61) goes no further than to assign Fletcher's portion of the play as Acts II. 1, 2, III. 2, V. 2, and Edith's part in Acts III. 1 and V. 1. In 1886 (*E. S.* IX, p. 22) he speaks quite positively, saying, 'It was really written by Fletcher, Massinger and Field with the aid of Jonson in one scene, IV. 2.' Boyle (*E. S.* VIII, pp. 54-7) sees the hand of Massinger (I and V. 1a), Fletcher (II, III. 2, IV. 2, V. 1b, 2), Field (III. 1, IV. 3), and Daborne (IV. 1). Oliphant (*E. S.* XV, pp. 353-4) suggests that the play has been written more than once. He thinks that it was written originally by the author of Acts III. 1 and IV. 3, rewritten by Fletcher, Jonson, and Middleton, and finally revised by Massinger in 1636. Bullen (*D. N. B.*) holds that a 'plausible view' is that the *Bloody Brother* was written in the first instance by Fletcher and Jonson and revised by Massinger on the occasion of its revival at Hampton Court in January 1636-7. Macaulay (*C. H. L.* VI, p. 156) says, 'probably four authors' and divides the play between Massinger (I, V. 1), Fletcher (II. 3, III. 1 (part), 2, V. 2), Field (III. 1 (except scene of Rollo and Edith), IV. 3), and Jonson (II. 1, 2, IV. 1, 2). On grounds of style Charles Crawford (*Sh. Jhrb.* XLI (1905), pp. 163-76) attributes it to Massinger, Fletcher, and Jonson. Sykes (*S. E. D.,* p. 219) finds 'no justification' for the allotment of any part of this play to Field.

The more general, and usually more convincing, tests of

tone, figures of speech, and vocabulary do not indicate the presence of Field, and metrical tests preclude the possibility of his collaboration. Act III shows 40% double endings and 20% run-on lines, which is conclusive indication that Field is not the author. If we exclude from these figures the scene between Rollo and Edith, which with 69% double endings and one run-on line could not be Field's, the figures are still decisive: 34% double endings and 23.9% run-on lines. The tests are equally definite for Act IV. 3—34.5% double endings and 35.8% run-on lines.

The question of the authorship of *The Faithful Friends* is one of the most perplexing in connection with the entire group of plays associated with Field. It was not entered in the *Stationers' Register* until June 29, 1660 (Eyre, II, p. 271). It was then given as by Beaumont and Fletcher. Fleay (*E. S.* XIII, p. 32) thinks Field and Daborne joint authors of *The Faithful Friends,* basing his opinion on likeness in authorship to *Honest Man's Fortune,* Acts II and IV, and on a date which Boyle has shown as probably incorrect. Two years later (*Drama* I, pp. 81 and 200-1), he gives all of the play to Daborne except Act IV. 5, which he believes to be the collaborative work mentioned in Daborne's letter of 11 March, 1614, to Henslowe. Chambers (*E. Stage* III, pp. 232-3) points out that this letter more likely refers to *The Owl.* Boyle (*E. S.* VII, p. 75) shows that *The Faithful Friends* belongs to a later period than had previously been supposed, and suggests Shirley. The allusion to the relation between Philip III and the Duke of Lerma (Act I, p. 124) is referred to as in the past, and so this allusion must have been made after Lerma's disgrace in 1618, or even more likely, after Philip's death in 1621. Oliphant (*E. S.* XV, pp. 331-2) suggests that the play is early Beaumont and Fletcher (c. 1604) revised in 1613-4 by Massinger and Field.[30] He divides it:

[30] Further study has only strengthened this opinion and led Oliphant to date a revision by Field as early as 1610-1 and a separate revision by Massinger in 1613-4 (*op. cit.,* pp. 353-68).

Beaumont.   III. 2b (from Arm.'s entry to Leon.'s), 2d (from Per.'s
             entry) ; III. 3a, c (from Bel.'s third entry to Roman
             Herald's entry) ; and IV. 4b (last 5 speeches), 5
             (perhaps Field).
Beaumont and Field.   I. 3 ; II. 1b, 2b (from Per.'s entry) ; III.
             3b, d ; IV. 1 (except one speech).
Beaumont and Massinger.   I. 1 ; II. 3a ; III. 2a, c ; IV. 3a (to the
             masque), 4a ; V. 2 (conclusion, B.).
Field.   II. 1a (first speech), 2a ; III. 1.
Massinger.   IV. 3b.
Fletcher.   I. 2.
Fletcher and Massinger.   II. 3b (from Mar.'s exit), V. 1.

Bullen, Gayley, Sykes, and Chambers have no suggestion to
make as to the authorship of the play. Sykes (*S. E. D.,* p.
219) holds that 'the most reasonable conclusion' is that it
is by none of the suggested authors.

Boyle's date, which seems the most plausible suggested,
precludes Oliphant's theory of Massinger and Field revision in 1613-4. Sixteen hundred twenty-one would put the
date of composition after Field's death. Even the year 1618
would mean that we should have to keep in mind Field's style
as shown in the *Knight of Malta* and the *Fatal Dowry* when
examining the work for his presence. Certainly there is
nothing in the style to indicate the writing of Field at this
period ; it is much worse than that of Field's first play.
Metrical tests lend no support to the theory of Field's
collaboration after 1618. Such tests show only a very few
scenes which might be attributed to Field at even the date of
Weathercock. They do testify to collaborative work in the
play, but I do not recognize the authors. It is true that some
expressions here and there through the play do remind one of
Field, but the evidence is too weak to be of any value in the
attempt to solve the problem of authorship for this execrable
play.

The problem of authorship in this play is very difficult,
but I do not think that it can be settled by attributing the
play to Field on evidence as inconclusive as that found.

As I have previously stated, the hypothesis has been

advanced that Field had a share in the revision of four plays. Fleay and Oliphant suggest Field as the reviser of *Cupid's Revenge;* Oliphant does not think Field had part in the original composition of *The Faithful Friends,* but supposes that he and Massinger revised the play. Professor Parrott mentions Field as the possible reviser of Chapman's *Bussy D'Ambois* and of *Timon of Athens.*

Cupid's Revenge was acted by the Queen's Revels company at Court in 1612 and again in 1613. Fleay (*E. S.* XIII, p. 31) says, 'This reviser was surely Field. No other author capable of such work is known at this date in connection with the Revel's children, and his peculiar careless omission of words shows in almost every scene.' He divides the play: Fletcher, Acts I. 1 (part), 2, II. 6, III. 3, 4, IV. 1, 2, 3, 4 (part), V. 1 (part), 2 (part), 4; Beaumont, Acts I. 1 (part), 3, 4, II. 1, 2, 3, 4, 5, III. 1, 2, IV. 4 (part), 5, V. 1 (part), 2 (part), 3. He thinks that Field has 'condensed and altered' in every scene. Later (*Drama* I, p. 188) he says the reviser is Field or possibly Daborne. Boyle (*E. S.* V, p. 75) says the play has been 'so altered that any conclusions drawn from the versification must be considered as mere guesses.' Later (*E. S.* VIII, p. 39) by means of metrical tests, he discovers a third hand in the text itself, though he is unable to identify the unknown author. Oliphant, after making one intricate division of the play with which he himself was dissatisfied (*E. S.* XIV, p. 84), claims in 1891 (*E. S.* XV, p. 321) to have succeeded in overcoming the earlier difficulty that he had experienced. In his new division, he gives to Beaumont most of that which he had formerly indicated as Field's. He makes the following division of the part in which he feels that he can name the author: Fletcher and Field, Act II. 6; Beaumont and Fletcher, Acts II. 3, 4, 5, III. 1, V. 1; Beaumont, Acts IV. 5, V. 4b; and Field, Act II. 1.[31]

[31] He now credits Field with I. 1a (to Leontius' exit), II. 1, 2 (with perhaps some Beaumont), 4, IV. 5, V. 1, 4b (from Timantus' entry to 'But leave you to Heaven'), (*op. cit.,* p. 351).

Many of the scenes in this play are too short for metrical tests to be very conclusive; but such tests are useful as indicators, though they must be considered in connection with style and content. According to metrical tests, Act II. 1 could not possibly be Field's work, for it has no double endings and 61% run-on lines. There is no reason to doubt this result after an examination of style and content. The fact that Act II. 4 contains an account of a lord at his toilet makes one think of Field, but the scene lacks the sprightliness and the spirit of pure fun which such representations have under Field's hand. Field's vain characters are ridiculous, but we do not scorn them; Leontius arouses our scorn and a feeling of repulsion. His preparations are largely given by report, and we miss the commendations and asides which add life to Field's scenes.

Chambers thinks that the type of revision present, that is the changing of the titles of King, Queen, and Prince to Duke, Duchess, and Marquis, necessitates no outside reviser and that Fleay's suggestion has led to chaos (*E. Stage* III, p. 225). Gayley (*Beaumont, the Dramatist,* p. 360) recognizes Beaumont in Acts I. 3, II. 2, III. 2, IV. 1, and V. 4. The critics, in general, agree pretty well that the play is the work of Beaumont and Fletcher. I see nothing to indicate that Field revised the play. The tone, figures of speech, and diction do not show that he took part in the composition; the stage directions are brief and very simple, noting only the entrances and exits and the most obvious changes in position. If Field had assisted in the revision of the play, he would not have neglected to equip each act with directions circumscribing the action and making the manner of the presentation unmistakable.

Professor Parrott, in *Modern Language Review* for January 1908, presents the idea that *Bussy D'Ambois* was revised, possibly with the aid of Field, for the Children of the Revels at the Whitefriars about 1610 and was carried to the King's company by Field. He points out a number of short passages and says, 'With hardly an exception, they add nothing to the poetic value of the play, but they do in every case add to its stage effects by inserting touches of humour, by linking a scene with what has preceded, or by furnishing a motive for what is to come, and by making the situation clearer to the spectator.' All this is true, but I do not detect Field's hand in the composition. The passages cited have nothing about them to indicate Field's writing, and there is no break in style at these points to indicate that a reviser is responsible for the lines. The friendly relation between Chapman and Field would have made it possible for the young actor to make practical suggestions as to the presentation of this play in which he was to act the title rôle. Aid of this nature might well account for changes; such as the cut of fifty lines at the beginning of Act II. 2, made possible by the shifting of Montsurry into Act II. 1, so that he became a witness of the King's pardon of Bussy, and the transfer of the dialogue between Monsieur and Guise from its first position after the catastrophe, to Act V. 2. The whole supposition is merely an interesting hypothesis, but I think that if Field were assisting Chapman in the revision of the play, his contribution was the suggestion of linking and motivation and not the actual writing of lines.

In 1923 Professor Parrott presented before the Shakespeare Association a paper entitled *The Problem of Timon of Athens.* In this paper he very ably supports the theory that *Timon* was begun by Shakespeare and completed by Chapman. He says, also, that 'nearly all the Chapman scenes show signs of heavy cutting.' He advances the following idea:

'I suppose, then, that the manuscript as it came back from Chapman was thoroughly overhauled, cut down, and patched up by some third writer, possibly by Field himself, and was then equipped with the elaborate stage directions that prove it was prepared for the stage.'

He cites Field as the reviser because of the old friendship between Chapman and Field and because of Field's knowledge of stagecraft. But he adds, 'The hasty work of the final reviser brought about a confusion twice confounded.' This is exactly what Field would not have done. The most distinctive mark of Field's work is the excellent technique shown. If Field had undertaken the job of revising the play for the stage, signs of hasty lopping would not have been left; the play would have gone from his hands in such a condition that it would have been at least a well-knit and successful stage production. Professor Parrott says, '*Timon* in its final form could never have been successful.' Such a statement in itself refutes the theory of Field's revision, and is inconsistent with his statement already quoted in regard to the type of revision of which he thought Field capable. *Timon* lacks the very linking together and clearing up of situation which we should suppose Field's contribution to give. Professor Parrott thinks that the reviser wrote these passages: Acts II. 2, 195-202, III. 1, 52-66, III. 3, perhaps III. 4, IV. 1, 35-40, and V. 3. The ground on which Field became the recipient of these lines is that they are certainly not Shakespeare, and not convincingly Chapman. But they are not Field. The vocabulary is not his: there are only two words in these lines which are frequently used by Field, *hum* (used twice) and *bounteous!* The fact that there is a mixture of prose, rhyme, and blank verse does make one think of Field. The occurrence of rhyme is rather frequent, however, even for Field, for in Act III. 3 there are six couplets in 34 lines of verse and in Act III. 4, nine couplets in 99 lines of verse. Although Act III. 3, 4 are quite brief for the application of metrical tests, these tests corroborate the other types of evidence and lend a certain authority to the conclusion that Field had no hand in the composition: Act III. 3 has 26.4% double endings and 11.7% run-on lines; Act III. 4 has 16% double endings and 7% run-on lines. These figures speak against the authorship of Field, for in no instance does Field have a greater number of double endings than run-on lines. I see nothing in the ten lines of Act V. 3 to indicate Field. The elaborate stage directions with which the play is equipped are very much in Field's manner. The use of speech in concert, so frequently mentioned in this paper as a device employed by Field, is used three times in Act I. 2, six times in Act II. 2, three times in Act IV. 3, six times in Act V. 1, and once in Act V. 4. The care for detail is evident, and in a few cases even the manner in which the action is to be per-formed is indicated: 'Enter Lord Timon, addressing himself *courteously* to every suitor' (Act I. 1); 'then comes dropping after all, Apemantus, *discontentedly,* like himself' (Act I. 2). This is quite in the Field style. I do not think, how-ever, that such evidence is conclusive proof that Field was the one who fitted out the play with stage directions, though he may have done so. Shakespeare himself, for example, often used speech in unison; and as I have previously pointed out, Chapman equipped his own plays with very definite stage directions and was probably the one who taught Field the advantage of furnishing a play with complete directions for acting.

As to Field's work as reviser, then, I feel that he had nothing to do with *The Faithful Friends* or *Cupid's Revenge,* and that if he were concerned in the revision of *Bussy D'Ambois* or of *Timon of Athens,* it was only as adviser to Chapman in the technicalities of stage production and not in the revision of lines.

Aside from the work bearing Field's signature, what com-position may reasonably be attributed to him? The evidence is satisfactory, I think, for the *Induction, Triumph of Honour,* and *Triumph of Love* in *Four Plays;* for Acts III and IV of the *Queen of Corinth;* Acts I and V of the *Knight of Malta;* and Act IV of the *Honest Man's Fortune.* Although the body of his work is fairly small, the quality is good enough to make Field a dramatist of more distinc-tion than has previously been recognized and to make us feel that his early death was a misfortune to drama as well as to the stage.

APPENDIX

Letter of John Field to the Earl of Leicester
Cotton MS. Titus B. VII.

Folio 22

The gracious grace of o^r Lord Jesus Christe be wth yo^w & fulfill wth his spirite all the holy desiers of yor hearte
Amen.

Howe shoulde I forgeate yo^w (my good lord) to whom I ame so many waies bounde in Christe, sith not onely I, but the whole Church do owe thankfulness vnto yo^w as the instrument both of my peace & libertie and of y^t. poore blessinge it enioyeth by my preachinge: Sutch a benefytte as I do p^rferre before my lyfe, w^thout wch my lyfe shoulde be vnp(ro)fitable: This is the cawse (my good lord) y^t I watch all oportunities, of doinge y^t dewtie, wherw^th I stande specially bounde vnto yo^w, still to stirre yo^w up, amiddest the many folde incombrances y^t followe yor lyfe, howe glorious soever it seme to be, yet compassed wth many feares, miseries & daungers. But if yo^w stande fast, & fainte not in y^t excellent hope, if yo^w walke wth yor God, wth an vprighte (&) a single hearte, and syncere affection to the Gospell of yor God, in a plaine p(ro)fession & full practise: doubte not (my lord) but he y^t hath hitherto so mercyfully supported yo^w, wilbe yor gratious & good God to th' ende. And howesoeu^er he trye yor patience by sundry crosses and afflictions, yet these trialls so many as they are & may be, shalbe so many arguments of the comfortable experience of his goodnes & favoure towards yo^w. Onelie praye y^t yo^w maye stand fast, & so I will praye for yo^w, that to ease yo^rselfe, yo^w vse no other meanes then are agreable to his will. The more Sathan rageth, the more valiante be yo^w

vnder the standert of him who will not be foyled. And I
humblie beseech yor hono^r to take heede howe yo^w gyve
yor hande either in euill cawses, or in the behalfe of euill
men as of late yo^w did for players to the greate griefe of
all the Godly, but as yo^w have shewed yor forwardnes for
the Ministery of the Gospell, so followe y^t course still. O^r
Cyttie hath bine well eased of the pester of those wickednesses & abuses, that were wonte to be nourished by those
impure enterludes & playes y^t were in vse, surely the schooles
of as greate wickednesses as can be: I truste yor hono^r
will herein ioyne wth them y^t have longe owt of the word
cryed owt against them, & I ame p(er)swaded y^t if yor
hono^r knowe what sincks of synne they are, yo^w woulde never
looke once towards them. The lord Jesus blesse yo^w

Novemb. 25, 1581

Yo^r good lordshippes most bounden

Jo. Feilde

Will of John Feilde.   38 Rutland.   P. C. C.

In the name of God   The sixtenth daye of February Anno
Dm̃ a thousand five hundreth eighty seaven   I John Feilde
of the cittye of London preacher & minister of the worde
of God in whose mercye & gracious goodness by and
throughe thonely meanes and merritts of my Lorde and
Savyour Christ Jesus is all my hope comforte & assurance
and in the joye thereof I willingly leave this worlde & all
the vanityes thereof & gladly comitt & commend my selfe
& familye with the wholle church of God to his greate
providence & gratious mercye etc.   And for those worldly
things all & whatsoever belonging unto me I give bequeathe
& leave all the same unto Joane my loving wyfe whom I
make my sole and onely executrix of this my last will and
testament assuring myselfe of her uprighte and motherly
care of my children & hers and christian disposition to deale
towards all my creditors & likewise to seeke to gett my

debtes in towards the discharge thereof as shall become her
to doe   And so I have caused this to be written the daye and
yeare abovesaid and pronounced and declared the same to
be mine onely last will & testament in prescence of those
wittnesses whose names are subscribed & of divers others
whiche then weare also present with me.

F. Edgrton   Stephen Brodwell
Andrewe Palmer   W. Charke

Probate granted 1st June 1590 to Joanna relict of deceased.
Further grant 9th Janry 1600 to Theophilus Feild
natural & lawfull son of the said John Feild deceased.

Will of Theophilus Field. P. C. C. 82 Pile

In the name of God The one and thirtieth day of July
Anno Dm̃. 1635
I Theophilus Bishop of Saint David's by the providence of
God in whose mercy and gracious goodness by and through
the onely means and meritts of my Lord and Saviour Christ
Jesus is all my hope comforte and assurance   And in the
joy thereof I willingly leave this world and all the vanities
thereof and gladly comitt and comend myself and family
with the whole church of God to his great providence and
gracious mercy   And for those worldly things all and whatsoever belonging to mee I give and leave all the same unto
Alice my loving wief whom I make my sole and onely
executrix of this my last will & testament in assuring myself
of her upright and motherly care of my children and hers
and christian disposition to deale towards all my creditors
And likewise to seeke to get my debts in towards the dis-
charging thereof as shall become her to do   And soe I have
caused this to be written the day and year abovesaid and
pronounced and declared the same to be my last will and
testament   In the presence of those witnesses underwritten

Theophilus Meneven̄

Witnesses. Roger Otes   Richard Nott   Thomas Lloyd &
John Rees & David Moyan

Probate granted at London 26th July 1636 to Alice Field
relict of the said deceased & executrix named in the said will.

Will of Alice Field.   P. C. C.   7 Goare

(NOTE. The will quoted below is especially interesting on account
of the London property listed.)

In the name of God Amen   The three and Twenteth day
of June in Anno Dm̃ one thousand sixe hundred & thirty-six
I Alice Feild Relict and executrix of the last will and Testament of the late right Reverend father in God Theophilus
late Lord Bishopp of Hereford deceased being verie sick
and weake in body but yet of good & perfect remembrance
praysed be god for the same and desirous to discharge that
trust wch was reposed in me in and by the will of my said
late Lord Bishopp deceased doe hereby for the setling of that
worldlie estate here lent me make my last will and Testament in manner following   First I doe will devise and
bequeath unto my sonne Playford Feild the Rever̃con and
Remaynder of yeares yett to come & unexpyred of all my
right and interest of in and to a Tenemt Messuage Taverne
or Burgage situate & being w^thin the parish of St Clements
Danes w^thout Temple barr now comonly knowne and called
by the name of the Nagges head Taverne and being in the
occupãcon of Anthony Rock Vintner or his assignes being
parcell of a lease wch I hould from Willm Farmer Esquier
and now demised at fiftie poundes [per] Annm̃ [per] the
said Playford my sonne yelding and paying thereout for his
parte of the reserved rent yerely being Twenty pounds [per]
Annm̃ unto the said Willm̃ Farmer or his Assignes the sume
of eight poundes yerelie at two usuall payments as by my
lease I stand bound   Itm̃ I give and bequeath unto Theophilus Feild my youngest sonne the Rever̃con and remaynder
of yeares yett to come and unexpired of all my right and

interest of in and to two Messuages houses or Burgages
scytuate & being in the parish of St Clements Danes afore-
said nowe in the occupacõn of Robert Mould or his Assignes
as they be now Devided being also percell of the said lease
wch I hould from the said Willm̃ Farmer & now demised
at the yerely Rent of fortie pounds [per] Annm̃ [per] the
said Theophilus my sonne yelding and paying thereout for
his parte of the said sume of twenty poundes [per] Annm̃
being the said reserved Rent unto the said Willm̃ Farmer
or his Assignes the sume of Twenty Nobles yerely at two
usuall dayes of paym[t] as I stand bound by my said lease
Itm̃ I give devise and bequeath unto my daughter Jane Feild
all the Reverĉon and remaynder of yeares yett to come and
unexpyred of all my right & interest in other two Tenements
Messuages houses or burgages situate in the said parish of
S[t] Clements Danes w[t]hout Temple barre and nowe in the
severall occupacõns of Thomas Haynes Cutler and . . . . .
Grocer as they be now devided being also percell of the said
lease and now demised at Twenty eight pounds [per] Annm̃
unto the said Jane Feild yelding and paying thereout yerelie
for her parte to make upp the said reserved rent of Twenty
poundes per Annm̃ unto the said Willm̃ Farmer or his
Assignes the yerelie sume of five poundes sixe shillings &
eight pence of lawfull english money at the usuall dayes of
payment as I stand bound   Itm̃ I give and bequeath unto
my daughters Alice Kemyes and Elizabeth Dowle to either
of them the sume of Tenne poundes   Itm̃ my will is and I
doe give devise & bequeath unto my eldest sonne John Feild
all that Castle and Mannor of Penhon in the County of
Monmouth together wth all the landes & Tenements leases
Rents services & appurterñcs what soever in as large &
ample manner as my Lord and I purchased the same of
Henry Billingsley Esquier   To have and to hold the same
Castle Mannor landes & premisses to him the said John
Feild his heires and Assignes forever.   Lastly I make and
appoynt my said sonne John Feild my sole executor to whome

I give all the residue of my goods plate debts and chattells
whatsoever towards the [per]forming of this my will and
helping and ayding of his said brothers and sisters and that
conscionable payment & satisfaction of his fathers and my
debts and accompts as his said father by his last will charged
me w^thall   In witnes whereof I have hereunto putt my hand
and seale the day and yeare above written.   Alice Feild
Sealed acknowledged and subscribed in the p^rsence of
Edward Kemeyes   signm̃ Anne Feild vid Roger Otes
signm̃ Sare Bateman

Admon. P. C. C.   August, 1620
Nathan Feild

The second day a Commission was granted to Dorcas
Rice otherwise Feild natural and lawful sister of Nathan
Feild late of the parish of Saint Giles in the Fields in the
county of Middlesex bachelor deceased having etc. to
administer the goods rights and credits of the said deceased
well etc. sworn.

(Translated from the Latin)

Admon. Act Book, Commissary Court of London.
March, 1632

On the 26th day of March 1632 Letters of Administration were granted to Anne Feild relict of Nathaniel Feild
late of the parish of Saint Anne Blackfryers London intestate deceased to administer the goods credits chattels etc. of
the said deceased etc. sworn etc.

Inventory of deceased's goods £45. 14s. 11d.

(Translated from the Latin)